A Greek Grammar
of the New Testament

A Greek Grammar

of the

New Testament

Curtis Vaughan
Virtus E. Gideon

A Workbook Approach to Intermediate Grammar

BROADMAN PRESS
Nashville, Tennessee

© Copyright 1979 • Broadman Press
All rights reserved.

4213-78

ISBN: 0-8054-1378-2

Dewey Decimal Classification: 225.48
Subject heading: BIBLE. NEW TESTAMENT

Printed in the United States of America

Preface

This workbook is designed for students who have completed one year of Greek. It is therefore assumed that they have mastered the essentials of the language. The course of study is divided into six units. The first unit contains an overview of the parts of speech. The second unit, with which the study of syntax begins, concerns the interpretation of the cases. The third unit consists of a single lesson on the article. The fourth, fifth, and sixth units concern, respectively, the verb, participles/infinitives, and clauses/sentences.

Interspersed throughout the workbook are reading assignments involving the translation of passages drawn from various portions of the Greek New Testament. In this way the student is introduced to different authors and different literary styles. Grammatical diagrams of example sentences have been employed in order to make syntactical relationships clearer.

The entire workbook is based on the assumption that a knowledge of Greek grammar is one of the indispensable tools of serious biblical study. Mastery of the grammar of the New Testament is therefore not looked on as an end in itself but a means toward equipping one to be a better interpreter of the best of all books.

The student may improve his knowledge of the Greek New Testament by various methods. One is to follow the Greek text while an English version is being read aloud, as in chapel services, family devotions, or church worship services. Another is to secure a recording of the New Testament and as it is played follow the Greek text. Still another means of advancing one's understanding of the language is to find someone to teach—wife, friends, fellow church members, etc. The discipline required in teaching another never fails to give the teacher insights which one would likely not acquire as a student in class. By all means a regular plan for reading the Greek New Testament should be followed. Without some such program one is likely to lose much of the skill developed in the classroom.

The following words of J. Gresham Machen offer sound counsel for the person who seriously wants to master his Greek New Testament:

> The Greek of the New Testament is by no means a difficult language; a very fair knowledge of it may be acquired by any minister of average intelligence. And to that end two homely directions may be given. In the first place, the Greek should be read aloud. A language cannot easily be learned by the eye alone. The sound as well as the sense of familiar passages should be impressed upon the mind, until sound and sense are connected without the medium of translation. Let this result not be hastened; it will come of itself if the simple direction be followed. In the second place, the Greek Testament should be read every day without fail, Sabbaths included. Ten minutes a day is of vastly more value than seventy minutes once a week. If the student keeps a "morning watch," the Greek Testament ought to be given a place in it; at any rate, the Greek Testament should be read devotionally. The Greek Testament is a sacred book, and should be treated as such. If it is treated so, the reading of it will soon become a source of joy and power (*Studying the New Testament Today,* ed. John H. Skilton, Presbyterian and Reformed Publishing House, p. 155).

Contents

UNIT I

The Parts of Speech

LESSON 1

The Parts of Speech

(τὰ μέρη τῆς λέξεως)

The parts of speech are the various classes under which all words used in speaking and writing may be arranged. Since every piece of literature is but some varying arrangement of these parts of speech, it is essential to know what they are and the part they play in the expression of human thought. They are substantially the same in Greek as in most other languages and may be listed as noun[1] (ὄνομα), pronoun (ἀντωνυμία), adjective (ἐπίθετον), verb (ῥῆμα), adverb (ἐπίρρημα), preposition (πρόθεσις), conjunction (σύνδεσμος), and particle[2] (παραθήκη). The first four of these (excepting the relative pronoun) express the great essentials of human thought; these, however, are often dependent for their full value upon the latter four, which may be called the thought-connectives. If the former are seen as the bricks that make up the substance of a wall, the thought-connectives (including the relative) may be likened to the mortar that

[1] Some grammarians prefer to use the word "substantive" and employ "noun" for both substantive and adjective.

[2] The article (ἄρθρον) is sometimes listed as a separate part of speech and indeed was generally considered such by the ancient Greek grammarians. There is much to be said for this, since the syntactical functions of the Greek article are unlike those of any other word. Separate treatment is given to the article on pp. 103-109 of this work. Ancient Greek grammarians also listed the participle as a separate part of speech. Nearly all modern grammarians treat it as a part of the verb system.

9

binds the separate elements into a single structure. They are the ever-recurring signs that point the thought onward or enable it on occasion to retrace its way so as to be clearer.

The Noun [3]
(ὄνομα)

Definition.—Dana and Mantey define the noun as a "vocal sound by which one designates a fact of consciousness. This vocal sound," they explain, "may be mediately represented by written symbols" (p. 62). More simply stated, a noun is "an appellation applied to a person, thing, or quality" (Robertson and Davis, p. 204). Dana and Mantey include prepositions, adjectives, pronouns, and the article in their discussion of the noun. We will use the term in its more restricted sense, and prepositions, adjectives, and pronouns will be discussed separately.

Function.—The various relations which the noun may sustain to the rest of the sentence are expressed in Greek by the eight cases. The cases will be studied in detail later, but it may be helpful to name here some of the more important noun functions. They are the following: 1) When it is in the nominative case, the noun may function as the *subject* of a sentence or a clause, being that part of the sentence or clause about which something is said. 2) When a nominative noun which is not the subject is used with a copulative verb, the noun completes the meaning of the verb and denotes the same person or thing as the subject. The noun used in this manner is called the *subjective complement.*[4] 3) A noun may function as the *object* (either direct or indirect) of a verb.

[3] The English word is from the Latin *nomen.*

[4] The subjective complement—some grammarians call it the predicate nominative—is not limited to the noun; it may be a noun, a pronoun, or an adjective.

When used as the direct object, the noun is normally [5] in the accusative case and receives the action of a transitive verb. The noun used as indirect object is virtually always [6] in the dative case and "indicates the one for whom or in whose interest an act is performed" (Dana and Mantey, p. 84). 4) In some instances a verb may be followed by two accusatives, one being the direct object and the other being the objective complement. [7] The objective complement (or predicate accusative), representing as it does the same person or thing as the direct object, is actually a type of apposition. 5) When one noun describes another noun to the extent of identifying it specifically, it is said to be an appositive modifier. The appositive noun will regularly employ the same case as the noun which it identifies, but sometimes the genitive form is used for the appositive regardless of the case of the word to which it is related. 6) In the vocative case the noun is used for direct address. 7) Those nouns which do not fit one of the preceding categories will for the most part be modifiers of one kind or another.

The Pronoun
(ἀντωνυμία)

Definition and use.—Robertson (p. 285) speaks of the pronoun as the oldest part of speech and as the most persistent in retaining its case forms. As its name suggests, the pronoun is a word used in place of a noun. There are many distinctive uses of the various classes of pronouns, but all of

[5] On rare occasions the genitive and the dative (and even the ablative) may be used for the direct object; cf. Robertson, pp. 506-12, 517-20, 539-41.

[6] The accusative with πρός or εἰς may sometimes be practically equivalent to the dative of indirect object; cf. Chamberlain, p. 34.

[7] Not every example of a double accusative will contain an objective complement, however. Sometimes both accusatives are direct objects; cf. Robertson, pp. 482-84; Dana and Mantey, p. 94.

them have one general function: to prevent the monotony which would necessarily result from the constant repetition of the noun. *Classes.*—There are twelve distinct classes of pronouns in the New Testament: personal (ἐγώ, σύ, αὐτός), relative (ὅς, ἥ, ὅ), demonstrative (οὗτος, ἐκεῖνος), intensive (αὐτός), possessive (ἐμός, σός, αὐτός), reflexive (ἐμαυτοῦ, σεαυτοῦ, ἑαυτοῦ), reciprocal (ἀλλήλων), interrogative (τίς, τί), distributive (ἀμφότερος, ἕκαστος), indefinite (τις, τι), alternative (ἄλλος, ἕτερος), and negative (οὐδείς, μηδείς).

The Adjective
(ἐπίθετον)

Definition.—The adjective may be described as a highly specialized substantive used to modify or to describe a noun. Though the line of division between the two is not always clear, adjectives are to be differentiated from nouns and are to be considered a distinct part of speech. They usually answer one of these questions: "which?" "what kind of?" or "how many?" Adjectives agree in gender, number, and case with the words which they modify.

Function.—Adjectives exhibit three primary uses: 1) As an *attributive* the adjective is used to modify a noun directly; that is, it gives an adherent description. If an article occurs with this construction—and as a rule it does—it immediately precedes the adjective.[8] The article occasionally is used before both the adjective and the noun, in which case the regular order is article, noun, article, adjective.[9] If the article does not occur at all, only the context can determine whether the adjective is attributive. 2) The adjective used as a

---

[8] As in ὁ ἀγαθὸς ἄνθρωπος or ἄνθρωπος ὁ ἀγαθός.

[9] As in ὁ ἄνθρωπος ὁ ἀγαθός.

predicate makes an assertion about the noun with which it is used. When used in this manner, the adjective may be linked to the subject by a copulative verb [10] or it may be in the predicate position [11] without a verb. [12] 3) Sometimes the adjective performs the full function of a *noun*. In such constructions the adjective always stands alone; that is, it does not have an accompanying noun with which it agrees in case, gender, and number. It may be found in the singular or plural, in any gender, and with or without the article.

The Verb
(ῥῆμα)

Definition.—The verb, since it is the heart of the sentence, is the most important part of speech for exegetical purposes. It has been variously defined. Dana and Mantey, for example, define the verb as "that part of the sentence which affirms action or state of being" (p. 154). In similar fashion, Nunn defines it as a word by means of which one "can make a statement, ask a question, or give a command about some person or thing" (p. 1). Robertson and Davis observe that "the two ideas in the verb are action (or existence or state) and affirmation," but they go on to say that "the one essential idea . . . is the affirmation" (p. 284). Chamberlain adds that "other parts of speech, e.g., the noun, the infinitive, and the participle, may express action, but the finite verb alone can make assertions" (p. 58).

In addition to person and number (the significance of which is obvious) a Greek verb has tense, mode (or mood), and voice. The tenses may express two relations: they may designate the time of an action as past, present, or future; and

[10] As in ὁ ἄνθρωπός ἐστιν ἀγαθός.
[11] That is, not immediately preceded by the article.
[12] As in ἀγαθὸς ἄνθρωπος, ἀγαθὸς ὁ ἄνθρωπος, or ἄνθρωπος ἀγαθός.

they may designate the kind (or the progress) of action as linear (i.e. as in progress), undefined, or perfected. In Greek tenses, kind of action is the principal idea. The time element appears directly only in the indicative mode. In the other modes, as well as in the infinitive and the participle, the time element is only relative if it appears at all. Mode indicates the manner in which the affirmation of the verb is made—whether positive and clear cut (indicative), hesitant or doubtful (subjunctive and optative), or in the form of a command (imperative). Voice tells how the action of the verb is related to the subject. The active voice represents the subject as producing the action. The middle voice represents the subject as acting with reference to himself—either on himself, for himself, or by himself. In the passive voice the subject is acted upon by an outside agent.

Character.—The distinctive nature of the verb may be made clearer by noting the most common classifications of it. For example, verbs are sometimes described as *finite* or *nonfinite*. Finite verbs, so called because they are limited to a subject by the personal endings, are those found in the indicative, subjunctive, optative, and imperative modes. Nonfinite verbs, sometimes called verbals, are the participles and infinitives.[13] Some grammarians, however, think that the participles and infinitives should not be called verbs at all but should be considered as two separate parts of speech.

Again, verbs [14] may be classified as *transitive, intransitive,* or *linking.* Transitive verbs, sometimes called verbs of incomplete predication, are those which require an object to complete their meaning. Intransitive verbs are verbs of

---

[13] In Robertson and Davis (p. 110) the verbal adjectives in -τός and -τέος are classed as nonfinite verb forms. This is technically correct, yet it must be admitted that the infinitive and the participle have special uses that put them in a class by themselves.

[14] In this book, "verb" will always mean "finite verb."

complete predication; that is, they make complete sense without an object. Linking verbs [15] are those which do not make predications at all but simply link the subject of a sentence with its predicate. The most common linking verbs are εἰμί, γίνομαι, and ὑπάρχω; but others are sometimes found.[16]

The Adverb
(ἐπίρρημα)

Definition and use.—Though often neglected as an inconsequential part of speech, adverbs have an important place both in the structure of the sentence and in the interpretation of the New Testament. Robertson and Davis define the adverb as "a fixed case-form of a substantive, adjective, or participle, numeral, pronoun or phrase used to modify verbs, adjectives, other adverbs or even substantives" (p. 246). They are used particularly to express relationships of time, place, manner, and degree, answering the questions "when?" "where?" "how?" and "how much?" In Greek, adverbs may occasionally be used even as substantives.

Scope of the term.—Some grammarians include under the term "adverb" all prepositions, conjunctions, particles, and adverbs proper. It is true that they all exhibit a close grammatical relationship, but inasmuch as prepositions, conjunctions, and particles have their own special uses, it is better to distinguish them as separate parts of speech.

The Preposition
(πρόθεσις)

Origin and definition.—It is generally agreed that the preposition began its career as an adverb; that is, prepositions

---

[15] Other terms for linking verb are "copula" and "connecting" verb.

[16] For example, καθίστημι, φαίνω, μένω, and other similar words, though they are actually intransitive verbs, are sometimes used as linking verbs.

were originally fixed case-forms serving as adjuncts to verbs rather than substantives. Robertson (p. 554) explains that at first the case-forms of the noun were sufficient to express its relation to other words in the sentence, but as language grew more complex, the burden became too great for the case-forms, and adverbs (prepositions) began to be used to make the case ideas clearer. Hence, the definition by Giles: "the preposition is therefore only an adverb specialized to define a case-usage." [17] Chamberlain, in line with this, calls prepositions "interpreters of the case-forms" (p. 112). Summers appropriately describes them as words "used to help substantives express their case function" (p. 32).

Function.—The definition of the preposition given above necessarily involved the statement of its primary use. It may be pointed out, however, that prepositions generally have a twofold function: they serve *as separate words or as parts of other words.*[18]

As separate words the function of prepositions is to help express case distinctions.[19] This, as has already been pointed out, is their chief office.

In composition with other words, prepositions have three uses: 1) They are used perfectively to give emphasis or intensity to a word.[20] 2) They frequently indicate direction,

---

[17] Giles (p. 341) illustrates the evolution of the adverb into a preposition by pointing out that forms like "στήθεσσι περί 'on the breast round about' would precede περὶ στήθεσσι 'round about the breast.' "

[18] The so-called "improper" prepositions do not have this double use. They are "adverbs used as prepositions with nouns and pronouns," but they are "never employed in composition with verbs" (Robertson and Davis, p. 249). Cf. Robertson, pp. 636-48.

[19] Cf. ἐν Δαμασκῷ (Acts 9:10). Without the preposition, the thought could be "in" (ἐν), "near" (πρός), or "beside" (παρά). The insertion of the preposition clarifies the idea.

[20] As in γινώσκω (I know) and ἐπιγινώσκω (I know fully), ἀπατάω (I deceive) and ἐξαπατάω (I deceive thoroughly), βλέπω (I see) and

location, or time.[21] 3) They sometimes completely change the meaning of a word.[22]

Interpretation.—A Greek preposition may be used to express one or more ideas. For example, παρά with the ablative is "from," with the locative it is "beside," with the accusative it is "beyond." This does not mean that παρά means one thing now, then another. The preposition is the same; the case varies and the meaning of the preposition varies accordingly.

The procedure in interpreting a preposition is as follows: 1) Begin with the root idea of the case. 2) Add the meaning of the preposition itself. 3) Consider the context. The result of this combination will be what one translates into English. It is important to note, however, that one translates the total idea, not simply the preposition.

The Conjunction
(σύνδσμος)

Definition and function.—The conjunction is an indeclinable part of speech which joins together two or more words, phrases, clauses, sentences, or paragraphs.

Classes.—The two kinds of conjunctions (coordinating and subordinating) make clear the relation between the two elements which they unite. The coordinating conjunctions join paragraphs, sentences, clauses, phrases, or words of equal grammatical value. The most common coordinating

---

διαβλέπω (I see clearly), ἐσθίω (I eat) and κατεσθίω (I eat up), διώκω (I pursue) and καταδιώκω (I hunt down). Cf. the English "burn" and "burn up," "hunt" and "hunt down," "seek" and "seek out," "follow" and "follow up," etc.

[21] Cf. ἔρχομαι (I go) and εἰσέρχομαι (I go in), γινώσκω (I know) and πρόγινώσκω (I know beforehand), ἔρχομαι (I go) and προέρχομαι (I go in front of or before).

[22] Cf. γινώσκω (I know) and ἀναγινώσκω (I read).

conjunctions are καί; τέ and its compounds (εἴτε, οὔτε, μήτε); γάρ; δέ and its compounds (οὐδέ and μηδέ); ἀλλά; ἤ; μέν; and οὖν. The subordinating conjunctions introduce clauses which are subordinate to some other part of the sentence. Examples of subordinating conjunctions are ἵνα, ὅτι, εἰ, ὡς, etc.

The Particle
(παραθήκη)

Definition and scope.—The term "particle" has never been exactly defined by the grammarians. Jespersen (p. 91), for example, uses it for all adverbs, conjunctions, prepositions, and interjections. Others (e.g., Robertson, pp. 1124-44) do not give such a broad scope to the term but in varying degrees limit it to one or more of those elements. Robertson holds that one must be arbitrary, to a certain extent, in dealing with particles, for, as he explains, it is not possible "to make a perfectly scientific treatment of particles without much overlapping" (p. 1143). In giving his own definition, he calls them "the hinges of speech, the joints of language, or the delicate turns of expression, the *nuances* of thought that are often untranslatable" (p. 1144). Colwell and Tune (p. 55) restrict the term "particle" to "a few short words that are not directly translated" (such as μέν, τέ, ἄν).[23] Dana and Mantey use the designation as a catch-all for "the odds and ends" in Greek grammar but "limit it chiefly to those words which do not properly belong to the regular classifications, such as conjunctions, adverbs, prepositions, etc." (p. 258). Margaret Thrall's *Greek Particles in the New Testament* is the definitive work on particles.

[23] The particle ἄν has no English equivalent. It often generalizes a word and implies vagueness, uncertainty, or indefiniteness in the sentences where it occurs.

Classes.—In the light of the foregoing paragraph, it is obvious that one must not be dogmatic in classifying Greek particles. It is felt, however, that a threefold division may be safely suggested: 1) intensive particles (ἀμήν, γέ, πέρ, etc.), 2) connecting particles (μέν, τέ), and 3) interjections (οὐά, ὤ, οὐαί, ἰδού, etc.).

Interpreting the Cases

Introduction to the Study
of the Cases

Word relations in English are denoted chiefly by prepositions and the order of words. In Greek the various relations which the noun may sustain to the rest of the sentence are mainly expressed by the cases[1]; however, prepositions, which developed much later than the cases, are used rather widely to assist the cases at this point.

There are only four or, in some instances, five case *forms*—the vocative is usually just the noun stem, or like the nominative—but there are eight clearly defined case *functions*.[2] The eight cases are: **nominative** (essentially the case of the subject), **genitive** (the "of" case), **ablative** (the "from" case), **dative** (the "to" or "for" case), **locative** (the "in" case), **instrumental** (the "with" or "by" case), **accusative** (essentially the case of the direct object), and **vocative** (the case of address). The object of this unit of study is to acquaint the student with the breadth of meaning in each of the cases and to develop his ability in interpreting case constructions which confront him in the Greek New Testament.

There are at least three things which the student must do in interpreting any given noun. 1) He must *ascertain its basic meaning.* 2) *He must identify its case.* 3) When he is sure of its case, he must then *determine,* so far as is possible, *the exact meaning of the case in its context.* All of the cases except the

---

[1] The English "case" is derived from the Latin *casus,* "falling." Nouns are conceived as "falling" in a certain relation to the rest of the sentence.

[2] Some grammarians deal with case in relation to the four or five forms, and recognize a number of functions associated with the forms.

vocative have a number of different usages, and in many instances two or more of these will fit equally well the word under study. It is the task of the interpreter to determine the one use that fits best the word and context under consideration. Often only one use will fit. The principal uses of the Greek cases are set forth in the following pages. The aim has been to state concisely and simply the leading idea in each case-usage, and this is followed in each instance by one or more examples from the Greek New Testament illustrating the point under discussion. The grammatical categories and terminology which are used are largely those found in *A Manual Grammar of the Greek New Testament* by H. E. Dana and Julius R. Mantey. Other grammars, however, have been frequently consulted, and occasionally terminology employed by one or more of them has been used instead of that found in Dana and Mantey.

A fundamental rule of language is that nouns in apposition with one another must be in the same case. The appositive, therefore, has not been included as a separate usage under each case. Special types of apposition, such as the "genitive of identity," have been listed, however.

Grammatical diagrams are employed to facilitate the student's understanding of the structure of the examples drawn from the Greek Testament. The basic scheme of the diagrams, adapted from L. R. Elliott's *Syntax in Diagram,* is as follows:

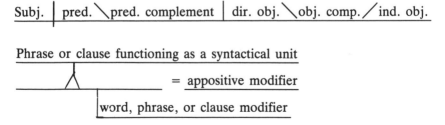

Subj. | pred. \pred. complement | dir. obj. \obj. comp. ╱ ind. obj.

Phrase or clause functioning as a syntactical unit

= appositive modifier

word, phrase, or clause modifier

LESSON 2

Nominative and Vocative Cases

(Dana and Mantey, pp. 68-72; Funk-Debrunner, pp. 79-82; Moule, pp. 30-32; Moulton, I, pp. 69-72; III, pp. 230-31; Robertson, pp. 456-66; Zerwick, pp. 9-12.)

Suggestions for the preparation of this lesson: 1) Read again the material on the noun, pages 3-5. 2) Study the material given below, observing carefully the examples drawn from the New Testament. Do not attempt merely to memorize the various classifications; aim first to understand thoroughly the basic force of the cases and then grasp each separate use. Study each example until you are sure that you understand it.

Nominative Case
(ἡ ὀνομαστικὴ πτῶσις)

The root idea of the nominative ("the naming case") is *designation*. The original function of the case was to give more specific identification to the subject of the verb. Robertson states it in this way: "Greater precision in the subject was desired, and so a substantive or pronoun was put in apposition with the verbal ending" (p. 457).

Of course as the language grew, the uses of the nominative multiplied. The New Testament exhibits the following:

1. *Subject nominative.*—The principal function of the nominative is to express the subject of a finite verb. Example: ὁ <u>πατήρ</u> ἀγαπᾷ τὸν υἱόν, "The Father loves the Son" (John 3:<u>35</u>).

πατήρ	ἀγαπᾷ	υἱόν
ὁ		τὸν

2. *Predicate nominative.*—The predicate nominative is a use of the nominative with verbs of being (εἰμί, γίνομαι, ὑπάρχω). (Quite often the linking verb is omitted, but in such instances it may be easily supplied from the context.) Sometimes the predicate nominative is called the "subject complement," because it completes the meaning of the subject and specifies the same person or thing as the subject. Example: ὁ Θεὸς ἀγάπη ἐστίν, "God is love."

Θεὸς	ἐστίν \ ἀγάπη
ὁ	

3. *Nominative of appellation.*—When a name or a title retains the nominative *form* irrespective of contextual relations, it may be called a nominative of appellation.[1] This is really a special kind of appositive which retains the nominative form even though it is used with a word in another case. That is, the word in the nominative form appears in that case form although the function would seemingly require some other case. In such constructions the retention of the nominative is sometimes practically equivalent to quotation marks, as in the following examples: ὄνομα ἔχει ᾿Απολλύων, "He has a name, 'Apollyon' "(Rev. 9:11). ὑμεῖς

---

[1] Many proper names are indeclinable and will therefore be found in the nominative form regardless of the function of the word in the sentence. These, however, should be classified according to their function. Thus, in the following example ᾿Ααρών (an indeclinable word) is a dative, for this is the manner in which it functions in the sentence: ἐστράφησαν... εἰς Αἴγυπτον, εἰπόντες τῷ ᾿Ααρών...; "They turned ... into Egypt, saying to Aaron ... " (Acts 7:39, 40).

24 A GREEK GRAMMAR OF THE NEW TESTAMENT

φωνεῖτέ με ὁ Διδάσκαλος καὶ ὁ Κύριος,[2] "You call me 'Teacher' and 'Lord' " (John 13:13).

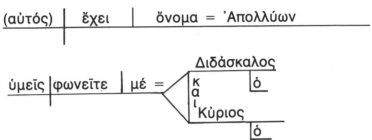

4. *Nominative absolute.*—When a word in the nominative has no real grammatical relation to the rest of the sentence, it is a nominative absolute. Dana and Mantey call this the "independent nominative"; others call it a "hanging nominative." This category includes:

1) The use of the nominative in those instances where the nominative form is left *suspended because of a changed construction.* This is an example of anacoluthon. Observe the following: ὁ νικῶν, δώσω αὐτῷ. . ., "The one overcoming, I will give to him . . ." (Rev. 3:21).

ὁ πιστεύων εἰς ἐμέ, . . ., ποταμοὶ ἐκ τῆς κοιλίας αὐτοῦ ῥεύσουσιν ὕδατος ξῶντος, "The one believing on me . . ., out of his inmost part shall flow rivers of living water" (John 7:38).

2) The use of the nominative in *salutations of letters:* Example: *Παῦλος*. . . τοῖς ἁγίοις τοῖς οὖσιν ἐν Ἐφέσῳ, "Paul . . . to the saints who are in Ephesus" (Eph. 1:1).

[2] Funk-Debrunner explain this as "a substitute for the vocative" (p. 79).

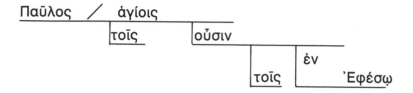

3) The use of the nominative in *titles of books*. Example: *Ἀποκάλυψις Ἰωάννου*, "The Apocalypse (Revelation) of John."

4) The use of the nominative in *exclamations*. This is "a sort of interjectional nominative" (Robertson, p. 461) and is a device for emphasis. Study the following examples: Ὦ *βάθος* πλούτου καὶ σοφίας καὶ γνώσεως θεοῦ, "O the depth of the riches both of the wisdom and knowledge of God!" (Rom. 11:33). τῷ θεῷ *χάρις* τῷ διδόντι ἡμῖν τὸ νῖκος, "Thanks to God who gives to us the victory!" (1 Cor. 15:57).

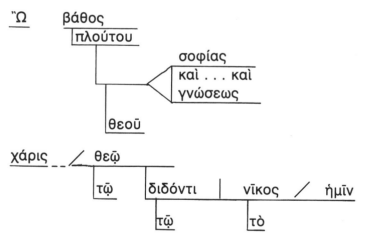

5. Many grammarians call attention to the nominative used "in place of" or "as" a vocative. This involves the employment of a nominative *form* (usually with the article) in

26 A GREEK GRAMMAR OF THE NEW TESTAMENT

direct address. Since the function is clearly vocative, it is perhaps better to classify these as vocatives.

Vocative Case

The vocative has separate case forms only in the singular number, and even in the singular some nouns do not have separate forms for the vocative.

Strictly speaking, since it is not affected by the structure of the sentence, the vocative does not enter as an element into syntax and is not a case. As a matter of convenience, however, it is best to treat it as such.

The root idea of the vocative ("the calling case") is *direct address*. Example: *ἄνδρες*, ἀγαπᾶτε τὰς γυναῖκας, "Husbands, love your (the) wives" (Eph. 5:25). Ἀναπολόγητος εἶ, ὦ ἄνθρωπε, "You are without excuse, O man" (Rom. 2:1).

ἄνδρες (ὑμεῖς) | ἀγαπᾶτε | γυναῖκας
                                |τὰς

ὦ ἄνθρωπε (σύ) | εἶ \ ἀναπολόγητος

Reading Assignment[3]

Translate the following verses, giving special attention to nominatives and vocatives: Eph. 4:4; 1 Thess. 2:20; Rev. 1:5.

---

[3] See Appendix II for suggestions concerning translating the New Testament.

LESSON 3

Nominative and Vocative Cases *(Continued)*

The assignments in the Greek Testament have to do with grammatical and syntactical studies. Various helps, in the form of parsings and brief grammatical notes, are given. Questions relating to specific points of grammar are inserted in order to guide the student in his study. These questions are to be answered before the class period.

1. Open your Greek Testament to 1 Thess. 1:1-3 and *read* the passage aloud. Now *translate* as much of it as you can without referring to lexicons, grammars, etc.

2. Having gone through the passage at least once without the assistance of any grammatical aids, go through it again using your lexicon to check the meanings of unfamiliar words.

3. Using the following notes, work through the text again:

Verse 1. θεσσαλονικέων is gen. pl. of θεσσαλονικεύς, – έως, ὁ. For its inflection compare βασιλεύς. θεσσαλονικέων is a proper name; thus, it is definite without the article.

The absence of the article in θεῷ πατρί suggests that these words were a fixed phrase in Paul's thinking. Paul's convictions concerning Jesus are summed up in the words κυρίῳ Ἰησοῦ χριστῷ: lordship, humanity, messiahship.

χάρις and εἰρήνη constitute the usual Pauline greeting (cf. Rom. 1:7; 1 Cor. 1:3; 2 Cor. 1:2, etc.). James (1:1), following the customary practice of the day, used the infinitive χαίρειν.

Verses 2-3. ποιούμενοι (vs. 2), μνημονεύοντες (vs. 3), and εἰδότες (vs. 4) give attendant circumstances of the action expressed by εὐχαριστοῦμεν (vs. 2), telling how, when, and why thanksgiving is offered to God.

Note that ποιούμενοι (vs. 2) and μνημονεύοντες (vs. 3)

27

are both present participles, although their forms differ. Can you explain this?

4. Give the case syntax of the following nominatives:

1) Παῦλος (vs. 1)_____

2) Σιλουανός (vs. 1)_____

3) χάρις) (vs. 1)_____

4) εἰρήνη (vs. 1)_____

5. Indicate the cases of the following words:

1) ἐκκλησίᾳ (vs. 1)_____

2) πατρί (vs. 1)_____

3) Ἰησοῦ (vs. 1)_____

4) ὑμῖν (vs. 1)_____

5) θεῷ (vs. 2)_____

6) ὑμῶν (vs. 3)_____

7) πίστεως (vs. 3)_____

8) ἀγάπης (vs. 3)_____

9) ἐλπίδος (vs. 3)_____

10) θεοῦ (vs. 3)_____

11) ἡμῶν (vs. 3)_____

6. What part of speech is πάντοτε (vs. 2)?_____ .

ἀδιαλείπτως (vs. 2)?_____. ἔμπροσθεν (vs. 3)?

_____.

7. Explain the accent of εὐχαριστοῦμεν (vs. 2).

8. Write your translation of 1 Thess. 1:1-3 here:

LESSON 4

Genitive
(ἡ γενικὴ πτῶσις)

(Dana and Mantey, pp. 72-81; Funk-Debrunner, pp. 89-100; J. Harold Greenlee, "The Genitive Case in the New Testament," *Bible Translator* 1 (April 1950), pp. 68-70; Moule, pp. 36-43; Moulton, I, pp. 72-74; Robertson, pp. 491-514; Zerwick, pp. 12-19.)

Suggestions for the preparation of this lesson: 1) Read again the material on the noun, pages 3-5. 2) Study the material below, observing closely the examples given. Do not try to memorize categories; strive rather for an intelligent comprehension of the material. Linger over each example until you understand it.

The genitive and the accusative are the most widely used of the cases. Both limit the meanings of other words. There are differences, however. For instance, the chief use of the genitive is to limit the meaning of substantives; the accusative limits mainly the verb. Again, the genitive answers the question, "What kind?" The accusative answers the question, "How far?" That is to say, the genitive limits as to *kind;* the accusative limits as to *extent.*

Robertson says the genitive case has the wrong name. The word "genitive" is from the Latin *genitivus,* (a translation of γεννητική), and means generative, productive. The Greeks called the case ἡ γενικὴ πτῶσις (from γένος, kind), suggesting "generic." They saw it then as "the case of genus (γένος) or kind," "the specifying case" (Robertson, p. 492). Dana and Mantey speak of it as "the case which specifies with reference to class or kind" (p. 75). The root idea of the

30

genitive is *definition* or *description*. Any genitive with a substantive is describing that substantive in some way; the context must usually determine how it is describing it. The genitive case is ordinarily (but by no means always) expressed in English by the preposition "of" or by the possessive form.

Genitive with Nouns

The following are the principal uses of the genitive when it modifies a noun.

1. *Attributive.*—The genitive may describe another word by denoting an attribute. This is the use of the genitive which lies closest to the root idea of the case. Dana and Mantey speak of it as the "genitive of description," but since all genitives describe, it is better to use the word "attributive" for this use of the case.[1] Example: ἐγένετο Ἰωάννης κηρύσσων βάπτισμα μετανοίας, "John came preaching a baptism of repentance (i.e., a repentance-kind of baptism)" (Mark 1:4).

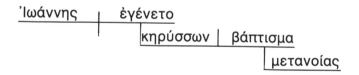

[1] Some grammarians call this type of genitive "qualitative." Zerwick prefers the designation "Hebrew" genitive. He explains that the scope of use of this type of genitive "in Biblical Greek is extended, owing to Semitic influence, to many expressions in which the Greeks used not a genitive but an adjective" (p. 14). He cites such examples as ὁ οἰκονόμος τῆς ἀδικίας (= the unjust steward) and ἀκροατὴς ἐπιλησμονῆς (= a forgetful hearer). "There is danger," cautions Zerwick, "that this manner of speaking may mislead those unaccustomed to it into reading some recondite sense into a genitive which in reality corresponds to some quite ordinary adjective" (p. 15).

2. *Possessive.*[2]—The genitive of possession describes another word by denoting ownership. This is one of the most common uses of the case, and requires little explanation. Example: ἐγὼ Παῦλος ὁ δέσμιος τοῦ *Χριστοῦ Ἰησοῦ* . . . , "I, Paul, the prisoner of Christ Jesus . . . " (Eph. 3:1).

3. *Appositive.*—The appositive genitive is sometimes called "genitive of identity."[3] It stands in exact apposition with the noun it modifies and describes that noun to the extent of identifying it in a specific way. Thus, the two words—the noun in the genitive and the word which it modifies—denote the same person or thing. No violence to the meaning would be done if one were to insert between the two words an expression such as "which is" or "namely." Or a comma might be placed between the two words, and the meaning would not be changed. Examples: κόκκος σινάπεως, "a grain of [which is] mustard seed"; τὸν στέφανον τῆς ζωῆς, "the crown of [which is] life"; τὸ σημεῖον Ἰωνᾶ, "the sign of [which is] Jonah"; τὴν δωρεὰν τοῦ Ἁγίου Πνεύματος, "the gift of [which is] the Holy Spirit."

[2] A special application of the possessive idea is the use of the genitive to describe a person from the standpoint of marital or genital relationship. The precise relationship—whether son, daughter, brother, etc.—is not stated but must be ascertained from the context. This is sometimes called the "genitive of family relationship." Example: εἶδεν . . . Ἰάκωβον τὸν τοῦ *Ζεβεδαίου*, "He saw . . . James, the (son) of Zebedee" (Matt. 4:21). (Literally it reads, "He saw . . . James, the (James) belonging to Zebedee.")

(αὐτὸς)	εἶδεν	Ἰάκωβον	=	(Ἰάκωβον)	
				τὸν	Ζεβεδαίου
					τοῦ

[3] Another term employed is "epexegetic (i.e., explanatory) genitive."

Observe that this is not the normal appositive construction. The normal appositive consists of two words in the same case, one being in apposition with the other (e.g., Παῦλος ὁ ἀπόστολος, "Paul the apostle"; also John 8:44, ὑμεῖς ἐκ τοῦ πατρὸς <u>τοῦ διαβόλου</u> ἐστέ, "You belong to your father, the devil"). The genitive of identity differs from this in that the word modified by the genitive may or may not be another genitive. Compare the expression, "the state of Texas." If this phrase were in Greek, the word for "state" could be in any case, depending on its relation to the context, but the word for "Texas" would be in the genitive. Observe the following example from the Greek New Testament: σημεῖον ἔλαβεν περιτομῆς, "He received a sign of circumcision" (Rom. 4:11). This could also be translated, "He received a sign, namely circumcision."

(αὐτὸς) | ἔλαβεν | σημεῖον = περιτομῆς

4. *Partitive.*—A word in the genitive sometimes indicates the whole of which the word modified is a part. This is ordinarily called a partitive genitive, though some grammarians speak of it as the "genitive of the whole." Examples: ἑκάστῳ <u>ἡμῶν</u> ἐδόθη ἡ χάρις, "To each of us grace was given" (Eph. 4:7). οὐδὲ Σολομὼν . . . περιεβάλετο ὡς ἕν <u>τούτων</u>, "Not even Solomon . . . clothed himself as one of these" (Matt. 6:29). ἕτερον τῶν <u>ἀποστόλων</u> οὐκ εἶδον, "Other of the apostles I saw not" (Gal. 1:19).

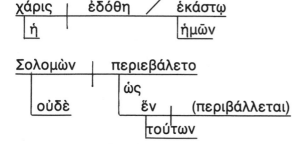

χάρις | ἐδόθη / ἑκάστῳ
ἡ | ἡμῶν

Σολομὼν | περιεβάλετο
οὐδὲ | ὡς
ἕν | (περιβάλλεται)
τούτων

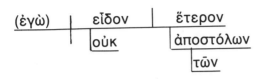

5. *Subjective.*—Some nouns are "nouns of action." These may often be recognized by their form (e.g., those ending in –σις or –μος), but nouns of action cannot always be identified in this way. If the form of the word does not provide a clue, the meaning of the word should make clear whether it is a noun of action.

A word in the genitive modifying a noun of action may sustain one of two relations to the idea of action in that noun: 1) It may denote that which *produces* the action or 2) it may denote that which *receives* the action. Only the context can make clear which of these meanings is expressed by a given construction. (Compare ἡ ἀγάπη τοῦ *χριστοῦ,* "the love of Christ," 2 Cor. 5:14; κατὰ τὸν καθαρισμὸν τῶν ᾽Ιουδαίων, "according to the cleansing of the Jews," John 2:6; τὸ κήρυγμα τοῦ *χριστοῦ,* "the preaching of Christ," Rom. 16:25. The first example, apart from contextual considerations, could mean either love *for* Christ or love *expressed by* Christ. The second example, removed from its context, means either cleansing *performed by* or *applied to* the Jews. The third example denotes preaching of which Christ is the *content* or preaching *done by* him.)

If the noun in the genitive *produces* the action, it is a subjective genitive. Example: τοῦτό μοι ἀποβήσεται εἰς σωτηρίαν διὰ τῆς . . . ἐπιχορηγίας τοῦ *πνεύματος,* "This shall turn out to me for salvation through the . . . supply of the Spirit [i.e., the supply which the Spirit provides]" (Phil. 1:19).

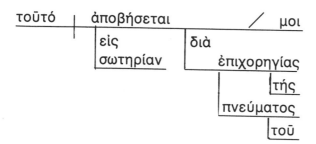

6. *Objective.*—If the noun in the genitive *receives* the action, it is an objective genitive. This construction may require "in," "to," "toward," "against," "concerning," etc. in translation. Examples: ἡ τοῦ <u>πνεύματος</u> βλασφημία οὐκ ἀφεθήσεται, "The blasphemy of (against) the Spirit will not be forgiven" (Matt. 12:31). ἔχετε πίστιν <u>θεοῦ</u>, "Have faith in God," (Mark 11:22).

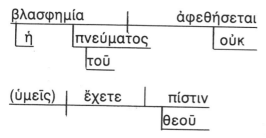

Genitive with Verbs

The genitive occurs rather frequently with verbs. The principal uses are as follows:

1. *Adverbial.*—The genitive used adverbially describes or defines a verbal idea by attributing local or temporal relations to it.

1) In an adverbial relationship the genitive may indicate *kind of time.* That is to say, the adverbial genitive may answer the question, "What kind of time?" (Compare the locative of

time.) Example: οὗτος ἦλθεν πρὸς αὐτὸν νυκτός, "This one came to him by night" (John 3:2).

2) In an adverbial relationship the genitive may indicate *kind of place*. That is to say, the adverbial genitive may answer the question, "What kind of place?" Example: πέμψον Λάζαρον ἵνα βάψῃ τὸ ἄκρον τοῦ δακτύλου αὐτοῦ ὕδατος..., "Send Lazarus in order that he might dip the tip of his finger in water" (Luke 16:24).

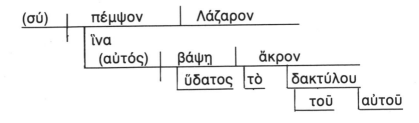

2. *Direct object.*—Some verbs—those, for example, which express sensation or perception (ἀκούω, hear; γεύομαι, taste; ἅπτομαι, touch; etc.); emotion and concern (σπλαγγνίζομαι, pity; ἐπιθυμέω, desire; καταφρονέω, despise; etc.); sharing (μετέχω, partake of, share in; κοινωνέω, partake of; etc.); ruling (ἄρχω, rule; κυριεύω, be master of, etc.); and so on—have a meaning which is related to the root idea of the genitive case. Such verbs may take their direct object in the genitive rather than the accusative case. Example: τῆς ἐκκλησίας τοῦ θεοῦ καταφρονεῖτε; "Do you despise the church of God?" (I Cor. 11:22).

Genitive with Adjectives

When used to modify an adjective, the word in the genitive restricts the qualifying force of the adjective to certain limits or completes the meaning of the adjective. (Dana and Mantey list this under "Adverbial Genitive" and call it "Genitive of Reference.") Some of the more common adjectives with which the genitive is used are μεστός (full), πλήρης (full), ἔνοχος (guilty, liable), and ἄξιος (worthy). The following sentences illustrate the use of the genitive with adjectives: βλέπετε . . . μήποτε ἔσται . . . καρδία πονηρὰ ἀπιστίας, "Take heed . . . lest there shall be . . . a heart evil with reference to unbelief" (Heb. 3:12). [ἡ γλῶσσά ἐστι] μεστὴ ἰοῦ θανατηφόρου, "The tongue is full of deadly poison" (James 3:8).

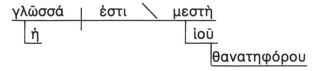

Genitive with Prepositions

The uses of the genitive with prepositions (such as περί, μετά, etc.) are sometimes difficult to define precisely. Most of them will have adverbial force. Example: εὐχαριστοῦμεν . . . περὶ πάντων ὑμῶν, "We give thanks . . . concerning all of you" (1 Thess. 1:2).

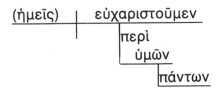

Genitive Absolute

"Absolute," from the Latin *absolutus,* means "loosed." An absolute phrase or word, then, is a construction loosed from the rest of the sentence. The genitive absolute is so called because it does not have a grammatical connection with the rest of the sentence. It does, however, sustain a thought connection. In the genitive absolute, there will be a noun (or pronoun) and a circumstantial[4] participle, both in the genitive case. Example: *ἐκβληθέντος τοῦ δαιμονίου, ἐλάλησεν ὁ κωφός,* "The demon having been cast out,[5] the dumb man spoke" (Matt. 9:33).

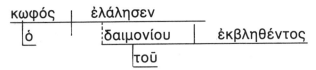

Reading Assignment

Translate the following verses, giving special attention to genitive constructions: Luke 4:1, 2; 5:3; John 2:21; 6:71; Eph. 1:16; Col. 1:22.

---

[4] See Lesson 35.

[5] This translation employs an English nominative absolute. It is generally better, however, to turn a Greek genitive absolute into an English clause. Thus, the above sentence could be translated, "When the demon had been cast out, the dumb man spoke." The context will usually make it clear what kind of clause to use, whether temporal, causal, etc. The temporal idea will likely fit more often than others.

LESSON 5

Genitive Case *(Continued)*

1. Review 1 Thess. 1:1-3.
2. Look over 1 Thess. 1:4-7; read the passage aloud and then translate as much as you can *without referring to lexicons, grammars, etc.*
3. Having gone through the passage at least once without the assistance of grammatical aids, go through it again using your lexicon to check the meanings of unfamiliar words.
4. Using the following notes, work through the passage again. Do not leave it until you are sure that you understand the grammar of the passage.

Verse 4. εἰδότες, a perfect active participle of οἶδα, should be construed as having causal force, stating the ground for the action of the main verb. οἶδα denotes intuitive knowledge (cf. γινώσκω).

Verse 5. The anarthrous constructions, λόγῳ, δυνάμει, and πνεύματι, emphasize quality or characteristic. οἷοι is a qualitative relative and could be translated "what quality (or kind) of men."

ὅτι may be either declarative ("how that") or causal ("because"). Frame thinks ὅτι governs the thought of verses 6 and 7 as well as that of verse 5. Of verse 6 he writes: "The sentence is getting to be independent, but ὅτι (vs. 5) is still in control" (p. 82).

Verse 6. μιμηταί is the root word from which is derived the English word "mimic." δεξάμενοι, aorist participle of δέχομαι, denotes not simply "receiving" but "welcoming."

Verse 7. ὥστε γενέσθαι κτλ expresses result. The terms Μακεδονίᾳ and Ἀχαΐᾳ have separate articles, indicating

39

that these areas are thought of as separate provinces. Compare the use of the same terms in verse 8, where only one article occurs.

5. Parse:

1) Ἰησοῦ (vs. 1)_____

2) θεοῦ (vs. 4)_____

3) ἐκλογήν (vs. 4)_____

4) δυνάμει (vs. 5)_____

5) πνεύματος (vs. 6)_____

6. Give the case syntax of these:

1) Θεσσαλονικέων (vs. 1)_____

2) πάντων (vs. 2)_____

3) προσευχῶν (vs. 2)_____

4) θεοῦ (vs. 3)_____

5) πατρός (vs. 3)_____

6) ἔργου (vs. 3)_____

7) ἀγάπης (vs. 3)_____

8) ἀδελφοί (vs. 4)_____

9) ὑμῶν (vs. 4)_____

10) εὐαγγέλιον (vs. 5)_____

11) ἡμῶν (vs. 5)_____

12) ἡμῶν (vs. 6)_____

13) χαρᾶς (vs. 6)_____

14) κυρίου (vs. 6)_____

15) μιμηταί (vs. 6)_____

7. Select the possessive genitives of verses 2-3.

8. Write here your translation of Thess. 1:4-7.

LESSON 6

Ablative Case
(ἡ ἀφαιρετικὴ πτῶσις)

(Chamberlain, pp. 32-34; Dana and Mantey, pp. 81-83; Funk-Debrunner, pp. 89-100; Moulton, I, p. 72; III, p. 235; Robertson, pp. 514-20.)

The ablative does not have a separate case form, and for that reason many grammarians do not recognize it as a case distinct from the genitive. Robertson, while insisting that the ablative should be recognized as a distinct case, admits that it "never had the manifold development of the Greek genitive" (p. 514).

The root idea of the ablative ("the whence case") is *separation* or *source*. In distinguishing between the genitive and ablative cases, one question should be asked: "Does the word under consideration indicate *kind* or *separation*?" If the stress is on kind, the word is to be taken as genitive; if separation is the main idea, the word is ablative.

There are other considerations which may help the student to distinguish these two cases. For one thing, the ablative is far less common than the genitive. Ablatives modifying other substantives are found infrequently in the New Testament. With verbs the ablative is rather frequently found, but not as often as the accusative, the genitive, or the dative. The ablative with prepositions is quite common, and the preposition often helps make the distinction between genitive and ablative clearer.

1. *Ablative of separation.*[1]—The ablative of separation is

[1] Some grammars recognize an "ablative of source," a construction in which the person or thing named in the noun modified by the ablative owes

the basic use of the case. The thing denoted by the word in the ablative is that from which something departs or is separated. Observe the following examples: ἦτε . . . ἀπηλλοτριωμένοι τῆς *πολιτείας* τοῦ Ἰσραὴλ, "You were . . . alienated from the commonwealth of Israel" (Eph. 2:12). παραγίνεται ὁ Ἰησοῦς ἀπὸ τῆς *Γαλιλαίας* ἐπὶ τὸν Ἰορδάνην, "Jesus comes from Galilee to the Jordan" (Matt. 3:13).

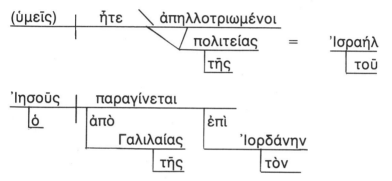

2. *Ablative of agency (means)*.—The ablative of agency tells the (impersonal) means or (personal) agency by which something is done. (The ablative is ordinarily used to express personal agency; the instrumental case is commonly used to express impersonal means. These distinctions, however, are not rigidly observed in the New Testament.) The ablative of agency often, though not always, employs ὑπό or διά. Examples: τὰ πάντα δι᾽ *αὐτοῦ* . . . ἔκτισται, "All things through him . . . have been created" (Col. 1:16). λαλοῦμεν . . . ἐν λόγοις . . . διδακτοῖς *πνεύματος*, "We speak . . . in words . . . taught by the Spirit" (1 Cor. 2:13).

---

its existence in some way to that which is denoted in the ablative. The meaning is often very similar to the subjective genitive and in other instances is not easily distinguished from the ablative of separation. We therefore do not include the ablative of source as a separate category.

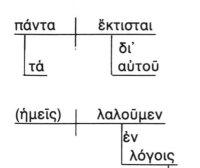

3. *Ablative of comparison.*—Comparison implies difference, distinction, or separation in *degree,* and thus logically fits the ablative case. This use of the ablative occurs with relative frequency in the New Testament. Example: μείζων ἐστὶν ὁ θεὸς τῆς *καρδίας* ἡμῶν, "God is greater than our heart" (1 John 3:20).

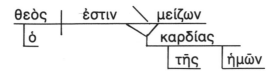

4. *Ablative of direct object.*—Verbs of ceasing (παύομαι), abstaining (ἀπέχομαι), missing and lacking (λείπομαι, ὑστερέω, etc.), and so on may take their direct object in the ablative case. This is because verbs of this sort are related to the root idea of the ablative case. (Cf. the genitive of direct object.) Example: Εἰ δέ τις ὑμῶν λείπεται *σοφίας,* αἰτείτω παρά . . . φεοῦ, "If any man of you lacks (comes short of) wisdom, let him ask from . . . God" (James 1:5).

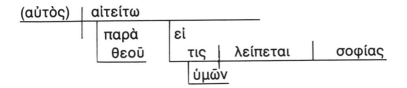

Reading Assignment

Translate the following verses, giving special attention to ablative constructions: Mark 1:5; John 13:16; Rom. 11:36; 1 Thess. 2:14; Rev. 21:2.

LESSON 7

The Ablative Case *(Continued)*

1. Review 1 Thess. 1:1-7.
2. Look over 1 Thess. 1:8-10; read the passage aloud and then translate as much of it as you can without referring to lexicons, grammars, etc.
3. Having gone through the passage at least once without the assistance of grammatical aids, go through it again using your lexicon to check the meanings of unfamiliar words.
4. Using the following notes, work through the passage again.

Verse 8. ἐξήχηται is a perf. pass. ind. of ἐξηχέω. (This word has a causative meaning in the present passage.) ἐξελήλυθεν is a perf. act. ind. of ἐξέρχομαι. The first article in the phrase ἡ πρὸς τὸν θεόν shows that πρὸς τὸν θεόν is an attributive modifier of πίστις. Observe the one article used with Μακεδονίᾳ καὶ Ἀχαΐα, indicating that the two provinces are thought of here as a unit, in contrast with the rest of the world. Compare the similar phrase in verse 7. ἡμᾶς is accusative of reference with ἔχειν. λαλεῖν modifies χρείαν. (Nouns and adjectives which have to do with authority, need, ability, fitness, etc. often take an infinitive modifier.)

Verse 9. ἐπεστρέψατε is an aor. act. ind. of ἐπιστρέφω.

5. What is the basic significance of the ablative? Write out the answer in your own words:

_____

_____

6. Give the case syntax of the following words:

1) θεοῦ (vs. 4)——————————————

2) πνεύματος (vs. 6)————————————

3) ὑμῶν (vs. 8, first occurrence)——————————

4) κυρίου (vs. 8)————————————————

5) πίστις (vs. 8)————————————————

6) ὑμῶν (vs. 8, second occurrence)——————————

7) εἰδώλων (vs. 9)————————————————

8) οὐρανῶν (vs. 10)——————————————

9) νεκρῶν (vs. 10)——————————————

10) ὀργῆς (vs. 10)——————————————

7. Write here your own translation of 1 Thess. 1:8-10.

LESSON 8

Dative Case
(ἡ δοτικὴ πτῶσις)

(Dana and Mantey, pp. 83-86; Funk-Debrunner, pp. 100-103; Moulton, I, pp. 75, 76; III, pp. 236-40; Robertson, pp. 535-43; Zerwick, pp. 19-20. In the study of the lesson, follow the suggestions given at the beginning of the lessons on the nominative and genitive cases.)

The root idea of the dative case is *personal interest;* that is, it accents one's personal advantage or disadvantage. Robertson explains that the dative is "sometimes used of things, but of things personified" (p. 536).

The dative is used more frequently with verbs than with any other part of speech. It is open to question whether it is ever used with prepositions. Robertson cites two passages (Acts 9:38; 27:8) where it is used with ἐγγύς and suggests that there may be an instance or so of its use with ἐπί.

1. *Dative of indirect object.*—The dative of indirect object is the use of the dative to indicate the one to whom, for whom, or in whose interest a thing is done. This is the most common use of the case.[1] Example: πάντα ἀποώσω σοι, "I will give you all things" (Matt. 18:26).

(ἐγώ)	ἀποδώσω	πάντα / σοι

[1] What some grammars call the dative of advantage (or disadvantage) is an intensive or specialized use of the dative of indirect object. (Strictly speaking, all indirect objects express either advantage or disadvantage.) In other grammars this is sometimes called the *dative of interest.* It denotes the person to whose advantage or disadvantage the action of the verb results. Cf. the English: "He lent *me* some money." An example of the dative of advantage (interest): ἔκρινα *ἐμαυτῷ* τοῦτο, "I determined this for

2. *Dative of direct object.*—Certain verbs take their direct object in the dative case rather than the accusative. (Compare this with the genitive of direct object and the ablative of direct object.)

1) Verbs that express *close personal relations* (e.g., ὑπακούω, to obey; διακονέω, to serve; προσκυνέω, to worship; ἀκολουθέω,[2] to follow; πιστεύω, to believe; etc.) may take their objects in the dative case. Example: σύ μοι ἀκολούθει, "You follow me" (John 21:22).

σύ	ἀκολούθει	μοι

2) *Verbs of speaking* may take their objects in the dative case. Example: εὐχαριστῶ τῷ θεῷ μου, "I thank my God" (Rom. 1:8).

(ἐγὼ)	εὐχαριστῶ	θεῷ
		τῷ | μου

3. *Dative of possession.*—The dative of possession is the use of the dative to indicate the person to whom a thing

myself" (2 Cor. 2:1). An example of the dative of disadvantage: μαρτυρεῖτε *ἑαυτοῖς* ὅτι υἱοί ἐστε τῶν φονευσάντων τοὺς προφήτας, "You are witnesses against yourselves that you are the sons of the ones having killed the prophets" (Matt. 23:31).

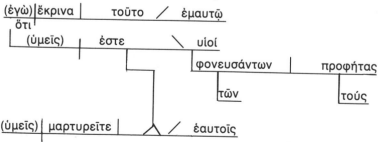

---

[2] Some grammarians prefer to speak of the object of ἀκολουθέω as being an instrumental of association.

belongs. (Cf. the idiomatic English expression, "Where is the *lid to the jar?*") This construction is particularly frequent in Luke's Gospel. Study the following sentences: οὐκ ἦν αὐτοῖς τέκνον, "There was not a child to them" (Luke 1:7). οἱ *σοὶ* μαθηταὶ οὐ νηστεύουσιν, "Your disciples do not fast" (Mark 2:18).

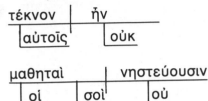

4. *Dative of reference.*—Sometimes the force of interest in the dative is reduced to the idea of mere reference. Two things are to be observed about this use of the dative: 1) The idea of advantage or disadvantage is not prominent in it. 2) Though it may occasionally relate to persons,[3] this use of the dative has to do mostly with *things.*

Example: ἀπεθάνομεν τῇ *ἀμαρτίᾳ,* "We died with reference to sin" (Rom. 6:2).

Note: In the following sentence some interpreters (e.g., A. B. Bruce in *The Expositor's Greek Testament*) think the underlined words are an instance of a dative absolute (cf. genitive absolute, p. 37): καὶ <u>ἐμβάντι αὐτῷ</u> εἰς τὸ πλοῖον ἠκολούθησαν αὐτῷ οἱ μαθηταὶ αὐτοῦ (Matt. 8: 23). If this is not a dative absolute, the αὐτῷ appears to be superfluous.

Reading Assignment

Translate the following verses, giving special attention to the dative constructions: Matt. 13:3; Mark 5:9; Rom. 8:12; Eph. 6:12; Col. 3:24; Rev. 21:2.

[3] Cf. English: "*To me* she is pretty."

LESSON 9

The Dative Case *(Continued)*

1. Review 1 Thess. 1:7-10.
2. Translate 1 Thess. 2:1-4, following the procedure set out in Lesson 5.
3. Notes on the text:

Verse 1. γάρ is to be connected with the thought of 1:9. Note the use of αὐτοί and εἴσοδον in both verses. τὴν εἴσοδον ἡμῶν κτλ is proleptic. The ὅτι clause, of which these words would normally be a part, explains and expands upon them. γέγονεν is a second perfect act. ind. of γίνομαι.

Verse 2. προπαθόντες, a second aor. act. ptc. of προπάσχω, suggests physical suffering. ὑβρισθέντες, a first aor. pass. ptc. of ὑβρίζω, has a connotation of insult, mental distress. ἐπαρρησιασάμεθα, a first aor. mid. ind. of παρρησιάζομαι, is always used in the New Testament in reference to preaching the gospel. πρὸς ὑμᾶς represents the use of an accusative where a dative of indirect object might have been used. This is a common construction in the New Testament.

Verse 4. δεδοκιμάσμεθα is a perf. pass. ind. of δοκιμάζω. Note the retention of the accusative of direct object with πιστευθῆναι, a pass. inf.

4. Distinguish between the dative, locative, and instrumental cases.

   1)   Dative_____

   2)   Locative_____

   3)   Instrumental_____

5. Give the case syntax of:

1) ἐκκλησίᾳ (1:1)_____

2) πιστεύουσιν (1:7)_____

3) θεῷ (1:9)_____

4) υἱόν (1:10)_____

5) αὐτοῦ (1:10)_____

6) κενή (2:1)_____

7) εἴσοδον (2:1)_____

8) ἀδελφοί (2:1)_____

9) παράκλησις (2:3)_____

10) πλάνης (2:3)_____

11) θεοῦ (2:4)_____

12) ἀνθρώποις (2:4)_____

13) θεῷ (2:4)_____

6. Parse εὐαγγέλιον (2:2)_____

_____

7. What case is φιλίπποις (2:2)?_____

Explain your decision:————————————————

8. Write here your translation of 1 Thess. 2:1-4.

LESSON 10

Locative and Instrumental Cases

(Chamberlain, pp. 35-36; Dana and Mantey, pp. 86-91; Funk-Debrunner, pp. 103-108; Moulton, III, pp. 240-44; Robertson, pp. 520-35; Zerwick, pp. 20-22.)

Locative
(ἡ τοπικὴ πτῶσις)

The root idea of the locative case is location or position. This idea is expressed in English by the prepositions "in," "at," "on," "among," etc.

1. *Locative of place.*—The locative of place is the use of the locative to indicate spatial location; that is, it locates within a spot or area. This construction ordinarily uses a preposition but may occur without a preposition. Example: ἦσαν ἐν ᾿Αντιοχείᾳ . . . προφῆται καὶ διδάσκαλοι, "There were in Antioch . . . prophets and teachers" (Acts 13:1).

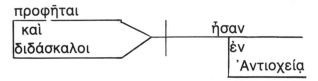

2. *Locative of sphere.*—The locative of sphere is the use of the locative when the expression is figurative or metaphorical; that is, it locates within logical limits, not within spatial or temporal limits. The locative used in this manner may occur with nouns, verbs, or adjectives. An example with a noun: ὑμεῖς τὰ ἔθνη ἐν σαρκί . . . ἦτε . . . χωρὶς χριστοῦ, "You, Gentiles in flesh, . . . were . . . apart from Christ" (Eph. 2:11-12). An example with a verb: δι᾿ αὐτοῦ ἔχομεν τὴν

προσαγωγὴν . . . ἐν ἑνὶ *πνεύματι,* "Through him we have our (the) access . . . in one Spirit" (Eph. 2:18). An example with an adjective: πραΰς εἰμι καὶ ταπεινὸς τῇ καρδίᾳ, "I am meek and lowly in heart" (Matt. 11:29).

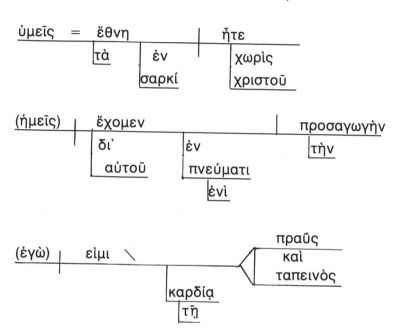

3. *Locative of time.*—The locative of time is the use of the locative to indicate point of time; that is, it locates within a succession of events. Compare this with the genitive (kind of time) and the accusative (extent of time). Example: τῇ *τρίτῃ ἡμέρᾳ* ἐγερθήσεται, "On the third day he shall be raised" (Matt. 20:19).

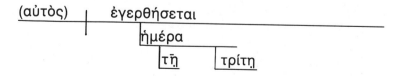

Instrumental
(ἡ χρηστικὴ πτῶσις)

The instrumental case embraces the ideas of both means and association (accompaniment). The meaning of the case is usually expressed in English by the prepositions "by" and "with." The New Testament exhibits the following uses:

1. *Instrumental of means.*—The instrumental is the normal case for expressing impersonal means. (Compare this with the ablative of agency.) The following are examples of the instrumental of means: οἱ μαθηταὶ . . . ἤσθιον τοὺς στάχυας ψώχοντες ταῖς *χερσίν*, "The disciples . . . were eating the ears, rubbing (them) with their (the) hands" (Luke 6:1). ἐγενήθητε ἐγγὺς ἐν τῷ *αἵματι*, "You were made nigh by the blood" (Eph. 2:13). τὸ δὲ ἄχυρον κατακαύσει *πυρὶ* ἀσβέστῳ, "But the chaff he will burn with unquenchable fire" (Matt. 3:12).

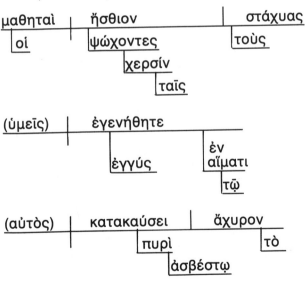

2. *Instrumental of cause.*—The instrumental of cause is the

use of the instrumental to present the idea of *cause, motive,* or *occasion.* Robertson says this usage wavers between the ideas of association and means. It goes behind the intermediate means to the original cause or factor producing a result. Study the following sentence: φόβῳ θανάτου ἔνοχοι ἦσαν δουλείας, "Because of fear of death they were subject to bondage" (Heb. 2:15).

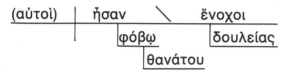

3. *Instrumental of manner.*—When the word in the instrumental presents an attendant circumstance of an action rather than the means by which it is done, it is an instrumental of manner. (It is sometimes difficult to distinguish this from the instrumental of means.) Observe the following: ἤμεθα τέκνα *φύσει* ὀργῆς, "We were by nature children of wrath" (Eph. 2:3). πᾶσα δὲ γυνὴ . . . προφητεύουσα *ἀκατακαλύπτῳ τῇ κεφαλῇ* καταισχύνει τὴν κεφαλὴν αὐτῆς, "But every woman . . . prophesying with her (the) head unveiled dishonors her head" (1 Cor. 11:5). ἐγὼ *χάριτι* μετέχω, "I partake with thanks" (1 Cor. 10:30).

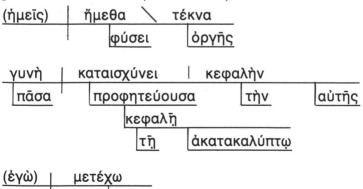

4. *Instrumental of measure.*—In the New Testament the instrumental of measure generally has to do with a temporal idea. Robertson (p. 528) therefore calls it "instrumental of time" and observes that it is similar to the accusative of time in meaning. Example: προσεῖχον αὐτῷ διὰ τὸ <u>ἱκανῷ</u> <u>χρόνῳ</u> ταῖς μαγείαις ἐξεστακέναι αὐτούς, "They gave heed to him because for (by) a long time he had amazed them with his sorceries" (Acts 8:11).

5. *Instrumental of association.*—The ideas of instrument and association (or accompaniment) are often closely related. (Compare the use of the English "with" to express instrumentality and "with" to express association.) Hence a very frequent use of the instrumental case is to express association. This use of the instrumental is often accompanied by the preposition σύν. The preposition may precede the instrumental or it may be compounded with the verb, as in the example following: συνεζωοποίησεν τῷ <u>Χριστῷ,</u> "He made (you) alive together with Christ" (Eph. 2:5).

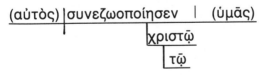

6. *Instrumental of agency.*[1]—Though the ablative with ὑπό or διά is the more usual way for expressing personal

---

[1] Compare the instrumental of means.

agency, the instrumental is occasionally employed. The verb will regularly be passive, and normally no preposition will be employed. Note the following example: ὅσοι *πνεύματι* θεοῦ ἄγονται, οὗτοι υἰοὶ θεοῦ εἰσιν, "As many as are led by God's Spirit, these are God's sons" (Rom. 8:14).

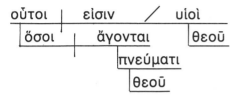

Reading Assignment

Translate the following verses, taking particular note of the locative and instrumental constructions: Mark 5:4; 14:30; Rom. 11:30; 1 Cor. 14:20; Gal. 5:18; 6:13; Eph. 1:1.

LESSON 11

The Locative and Instrumental Cases
(Continued)

1. Review 1 Thess. 2:1-4.
2. Translate 1 Thess. 2:5-8, following the instructions given in Lesson 5.
3. Notes on the text:

Verse 5. The γάρ of this verse resumes the γάρ of verse 3. What is stated in verses 3 and 4 concerned Paul's ministry generally; what is stated in verses 5ff. applies that general statement to the apostle's experience in Thessalonica (note καθὼς οἴδατε, vs. 5). προφάσει suggests here "the giving of a reason which is plausible in itself, but which is not the real reason. It is only a pretext" (Morris, *Tyndale*, p. 46). Paul's point is that he "did not use his message as a foil to cover selfish purposes" (Frame, p.98).

Verse 7. δυνάμενοι is a participle having concessive force: "although we were able." βάρει literally means "weight" or "burden." From this idea the meaning in this context may pass over to "burdensome" (KJV) or "authority" (ASV). NEB: "although as Christ's envoys we might have made our weight felt." ἐάν probably adds only indefiniteness to the statement and is thus equivalent to ἄν.

Verse 8. εὐδοκοῦμεν is an impf. act. ind. of εὐδοκέω. μεταδοῦναι is an aor. act. inf. of μεταδίδωμι.

4. Define:

1) Locative—————————————————————

2) Instrumental—————————————————————

60

5. Give the case and syntax of:

1) φιλίπποις (vs. 2)_____

2) θεῷ (vs. 2)_____

3) ἀγῶνι (vs. 2)_____

4) δόλῳ (vs. 3)_____

5) λόγῳ (vs. 5)_____

6) κολακείας (vs. 5)_____

7) προφάσει (vs. 5)_____

8) πλεονεξίας (vs. 5)_____

9) θεός (vs. 5)_____

10) μάρτυς (vs. 5)_____

11) βάρει (vs. 7)_____

12) ἀπόστολοι (vs. 7)_____

13) χριστοῦ (vs. 7)_____

14) νήπιοι (vs. 7)_____

15) ὑμῶν (vs. 8)_____

16) ὑμῖν (vs. 8)_____

17) ἡμῖν (vs. 8)_____

6. Write your own translation of 1 Thess. 2:5-8.

LESSON 12

Accusative Case
(ἡ αἰτιατικὴ πτῶσις)

(Dana and Mantey, pp. 91-95; Funk-Debrunner, pp. 82-89; Moulton, III. pp. 244-48; Robertson, pp. 466-91; Zerwick, pp. 23-26.)

The root idea of the accusative, the most widely used of all the Greek cases, is limitation. It limits as to extent, duration, direction, and so on.

1. *Accusative of direct object.*—When a noun in the accusative case receives the action of a transitive verb, it is an accusative of direct object.[1] Example: *ἀλήθειαν* λέγω, "I speak truth" (John 8:46).

(ἐγὼ)	λέγω	ἀλήθειαν

---

[1] The *cognate accusative* is a special type of direct object. It differs from the ordinary object in that the verb and its object are derived from the same root. It is sometimes a device for emphasis; often, however, it is simply used for stylistic effect. Essentially the cognate accusative repeats and explains more fully the idea expressed by the verb. (Cf. English, "to do a deed," "to work a work," "to sing a song," etc.) Examples of the cognate accusative follow: ἐφοβήθησαν φόβον μέγαν, "They feared (with) a great fear" (Mark 4:41). ἐάν τις ἴδῃ τὸν ἀδελφὸν αὐτοῦ ἁμαρτάνοντα *ἁμαρτίαν* . . . αἰτήσει, "If anyone see his brother sinning a sin . . . he shall ask" (1 John 5:16).

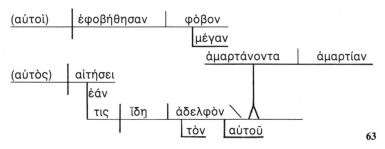

2. Adverbial accusative.—The adverbial accusative is the use of the accusative to modify or limit a verb in an indirect way. "It limits by indicating a fact indirectly related to the action rather than an object directly affected by the action" (Dana and Mantey, p. 93). In this construction the accusative functions as an adverbial modifier. Four types may be distinguished:

1) The adverbial accusative may express *measure,* answering the questions "How far?" (accusative of extent of space) or "How long?" (accusative of extent of time). The latter is more frequent in the New Testament than the former. Example: εἶδον τὰ ἔργα μου *τεσσαράκοντα ἔτη,* "They saw my works forty years" (Heb. 3:9f).

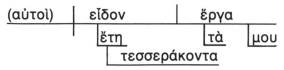

2) The adverbial accusative may express *manner,* answering the question "How?". Example: *δωρεὰν* ἐλάβετε, *δωρεὰν* δότε, "Freely (as a gift) you received, freely give" (Matt. 10:8).

3) The adverbial accusative may express reference, answering the question "With reference to what?"[2] Example:

---

[2] The accusative used as "subject" of the infinitive is properly called an accusative of reference. Example: ἐξελέξατο ἡμᾶς . . . εἶναι *ἡμᾶς* ἁγίους, "He chose us . . . that we should be holy" (Eph. 1:4).

πᾶς ὁ ἀγωνιζόμενος *πάντα* ἐγκρατεύεται, "Everyone who participates in an athletic contest exercises self-control in (with reference to) all things" (1 Cor. 9:25).

4) An adverbial accusative, accompanied by εἰς, ἐπί, or πρός, may sometimes express goal or *termination*.[3] (This, however, does not mean that in every instance in which these prepositions are used the construction is to be construed as terminal.) The terminal accusative is ordinarily employed with verbs of motion. Example: κατήντησεν εἰς *Δέρβην* καὶ εἰς *Λύστραν*, "He went down to Derbe and to Lystra" (Acts 16:1).

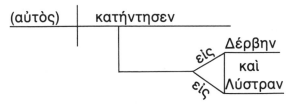

[3] Sometimes the terminal accusative, especially when used with a verb of speaking, is practically equivalent to a dative of indirect object, as in the example following: ἐκηρύξαμεν εἰς *ὑμᾶς* τὸ εὐαγγέλιον τοῦ θεοῦ, "We preached to you the gospel of God" (1 Thess. 2:9).

3. *Double accusative.*—The double accusative is the use of two accusatives with verbs that require more than one object (or other qualifying accusative) to complete their meaning.

1) The two accusatives may express a personal and an impersonal object (accusative of the *person* and accusative of the *thing*). Example: ἐκεῖνος ὑμᾶς διδάξει <u>πάντα</u>, "That one will teach you all things" (John 14:26).[4]

2) The two accusatives may express a direct object and a predicate object. (The predicate object is really a sort of appositive. It might be called an "object complement," because it completes the meaning of the object and specifies the same person or thing as the object. Compare the predicate nominative.) Sometimes εἰς will occur with the predicate object. The following is an example of a direct object and a predicate object: οὐκέτι λέγω <u>ὑμᾶς δούλους</u>, "No longer do I call you slaves" (John 15:15).

(ἐγὼ)	λέγω	ὑμᾶς \ δούλους
	οὐκέτι	

3) The two accusatives may occur with verbs for oath-taking. Some grammarians (Dana and Mantey, for example) make this a separate category, but it is really a form of the double accusative. (One of these accusatives is somewhat like the adverbial accusative of reference.)

---

[4] "Ask" and "lead" are the only English verbs taking both an accusative of the person and an accusative of the thing: "I asked *him* his *name*." "He led *them* a lively *chase*." "She leads *him* a dog's *life*."

Example: ὁρκίζω *σε* τὸν *θεόν,* "I adjure you by God" (Mark 5:7).

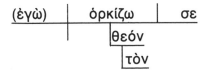

4. *Accusative absolute.*—When the word in the accusative has no direct grammatical connection with the remainder of the sentence, it is an accusative absolute (i.e., an accusative "loosed from" the rest of the sentence). This construction, which may occur with or without a participle, is very rare in the New Testament. Example: . . . δώῃ ὑμῖν πνεῦμα σοφίας . . . *πεφωτισμένους* τοὺς ὀφθαλμοὺς τῆς καρδίας ὑμῶν, " . . . that he may give to you the Spirit of wisdom . . . , the eyes of your heart being enlightened" (Eph. 1:17f).

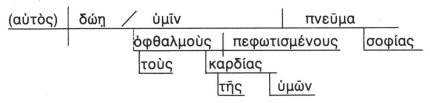

Reading Assignment

Translate the following verses, giving special attention to the accusative constructions: Matt. 20:6; John 1:14; James 5:10; 1 Pet. 5:2.

LESSON 13

The Accusative Case *(Continued)*

1. Review 1 Thess. 2:5-8.
2. Translate 1 Thess. 2:9-12, following the procedure set out in Lesson 5.
3. Notes on the text:

Verse 9. μνημονεύετε, which so far as its form is concerned, could be either indicative or imperative, should probably be understood here as an indicative (cf. οἴδατε, vs. 11). Note the case of κόπον and μόχθον. Everywhere else in Paul's writings μνημονεύω is used with the genitive case (cf. 1:3). πρός and τό are to be taken with ἐπιβαρῆσαι. The entire construction expresses purpose: "to the end that we might not burden any one of you." Robertson comments that πρός with the articular infinitive to express purpose is used by Paul only four times (*W.P.*, vol. IV, p. 19). ἐκηρύξαμεν is an aor. act. ind. of κηρύσσω.

Verses 10, 11. ὡς (first two occurrences in vss. 10, 11) is to be translated "how," being practically equivalent to πῶς used in indirect questions (cf. Arndt and Gingrich, meaning I, 2, d., p. 905).

Between the words ὡς and ἵνα (vs. 11) we must supply the main verb from the context. Some suggest παρεκαλοῦμεν ("urged"), some ἐνουθετοῦμεν ("admonished"), others ἐγενήθημεν ("became"). Frame resolves the problem by translating the first participle in verse 12 as having indicative force. The other two are understood as adding attendant circumstances: "As you know, we were urging you individ-

68

ually, as a father his own children, both by encouragement and by solemn appeal, to walk, etc."

Verse 12. εἰς τό with an infinitive is a common construction for expressing either purpose or result. Here εἰς τὸ περιπατεῖν expresses purpose: "to the end that you should walk, etc."

4. Give the case and syntax of the following:

1) δόξαν (vs. 6)_____

2) τέκνα (vs. 7)_____

3) ψυχάς (vs. 8)_____

4) κόπον (vs. 9)_____

5) νυκτός (vs. 9)_____

6) ἡμέρας (vs. 9)_____

7) τινα (vs. 9)_____

8) ὑμᾶς (vs. 9)_____

9) εὐαγγέλιον (vs. 9)_____

10) ὑμῖν (vs. 10)_____

11) ὑμᾶς (vs. 12, first occurrence)_____

12) ὑμᾶς (vs. 12, second occurrence)_____

13) βασιλείαν (vs. 12)_____

5. What part of speech is ἑαυτῶν (vs. 8)?_____

Explain its case————————————————————————

6. Select and parse the non-finite verbs of verses 9-12.

7. Select and parse the genitive-ablative forms of verses 9-12.

8. Write here your own translation of 1 Thess. 2:9-12:

LESSON 14

Translation and Syntax

1. Translate 1 Thess. 2:13-16.
2. Notes on the text:

Verse 13. The καί in διὰ τοῦτο καὶ ἡμεῖς is to be construed with ἡμεῖς. The idea then is "we as well as you" (Frame, p. 106) or "we on our part" (Milligan, p. 28). Some see this as evidence that Paul was replying to a letter from the Thessalonians in which they referred to *their* thanksgiving. The idea then is, "We give thanks just as you say that you do." Another alternative is to connect καί with διὰ τοῦτο: "Another reason why we constantly thank God" *(Jerusalem Bible).* ὅτι may be translated "that" (introducing the substance of the thanksgiving) or "because" (giving the reason for the thanksgiving). παραλαβόντες speaks of outward reception; ἐδέξασθε carries the notion of inward welcome. παρ' ἡμῶν, denoting the *intermediate* source of the message, is to be construed with παραλαβόντες. Τοῦ θεοῦ, pointing up the *real* source, is a kind of explanatory addition (Milligan). (Most of the versions take τοῦ θεοῦ as a simple possessive genitive: "*God's* message.") The antecedent of ὅς is λόγον. Arndt and Gingrich explain that the middle of ἐνεργέω is regularly used in the New Testament when the subject is impersonal. But Milligan prefers to take ἐνεργεῖται as passive, "is set in operation." This, he says, brings out more clearly the divine agency that is at work.

Verse 14. ἐπάθετε is an aor. act. ind. of πάσχω.

Verse 15. ἀποκτεινάντων is an aor. act. pct. of ἀποκτείνω.

Verse 16. σωθῶσιν is an aor. pass. subj. of σώζω. The

infinitive εἰς τὸ ἀναπληρῶσαι expresses purpose. "The obstinacy of the Jews is viewed as an element in the divine plan" (Frame). ἔφθασεν is an aor. act. ind. of φθάνω. The tense is gnomic in force (see Lesson 33, section 2) and stresses the certainity of the punishment awaiting unbelievers. εἰς τέλος may denote either "at last" or "to the uttermost." It is difficult to decide between the two. Conybeare, with less likelihood, translates it "to destroy them" or "to make an end of them."

3. Give the case and syntax of the following:

1) ἡμεῖς (vs. 13)_____

2) θεῷ (vs. 13)_____

3) ἀκοῆς (vs. 13)_____

4) ἡμῶν (vs. 13)_____

5) θεοῦ (vs. 13, first occurrence)_____

6) λόγον (vs. 13, second & third occurrences)——

_____

7) ἀνθρώπων (vs. 13)_____

8) ὑμῖν (vs. 13)_____

9) μιμηταί (vs. 14)_____

10) ἐκκλησιῶν (vs. 14)_____

11) Ἰουδαίᾳ (vs. 14)_____

12) χριστῷ (vs. 14)_____

13) συμφυλετῶν (vs. 14)_____

14) προφήτας (vs. 15)_____

15) θεῷ (vs. 15)_____

16) ἀνθρώποις (vs. 15)_____

17) τέλος (vs. 16)_____

4. Select and parse the first declension nouns of 2:13-16.

5. Select and parse the infinitives of 2:13-16.

6. Write here your own translation of 1 Thess. 2:13-16.

LESSON 15

Translation and Syntax

1. Translate 1 Thess. 2:17-20, following the instructions given at the beginning of Lesson 5.

2. Notes on the text:

Verse 17. δέ introduces a contrast between Paul (ἡμεῖς) and the unbelieving Jews (vv. 14, 15). ἐσπουδάσαμεν is an aor. act. ind. of σπουδάζω, a word which combines the ideas of urgency and earnestness. περισσοτέρως, a comparative adverb, seems to have elative sense in this passage (cf. rendering: "extremely"). Moffatt and others, however, retain the comparative force: "we were *the more eager* to see you."

Verse 18. διότι should here be translated "because" rather than "wherefore." ἠθελήσαμεν is an aor. act. ind. of θέλω. The seeming irregularity of the augment and the presence of η before the tense suffix are accounted for by the fact that this verb sometimes used the stem ἐθελέω. καὶ . . .καὶ (first two occurrences) may mean "both. . .and." Others prefer to read the first καί separately, understanding it in the sense of "and that" or "and what is more." ἅπαξ καὶ δίς (literally, "once and twice") is an idiomatic phrase meaning something like "more than once" (Morris) or "repeatedly" (Frame). ἐνέκοψεν is an aor. act. ind. of ἐνκόπτω (ἐγκόπτω). Note the placement of the augment between the prepositional prefix and the verb stem. The context suggests that καί (third occurrence) is adversative in force.

Verses 19, 20. These verses appear to be a reply to the accusation that Paul had no interest in the Thessalonians. He asserts that, quite to the contrary, they will be his gift to the Lord at his coming. The language contains an allusion to the custom of giving a wreath to a king who visited one's village. τίς is taken by most of the versions to mean "what," but Frame prefers "who." καύχησις, which denotes a joy both inwardly felt and outwardly expressed, takes on in this context the connotation of boasting. "Crown of boasting" is a crown in which one makes his boast. καί before ὑμεῖς is ascensive—"*even* you."

παρουσία, an important word used in the New Testament for the second coming of Jesus, literally means "presence." From that it came to mean "arrival," that is, "coming to be present." In secular literature it was used of the arrival or visit of a ruler to a province or city.

γάρ (vs. 20) has the sense of "indeed."

3. Parse the following words and indicate the basic idea of the tense of each word.

    1) ἀπορφανισθέντες (vs. 17)_____

    2) ἰδεῖν (vs. 17)_____

    3) ἐλθεῖν (vs. 18)_____

4. Give the case and syntax of the following:

    1) Ἡμεῖς (vs. 17)_____

    2) ὥρας (vs. 17)_____

    3) προσώπῳ (vs. 17)_____

    4) ὑμᾶς (vs. 18)_____

    5) Σατανᾶς (vs. 18)_____

    6) αὐτοῦ (vs. 19)_____

7) παρουσία (vs. 19)_____

8) δόξα (vs. 20)_____

5. Decline Σατανᾶς. If help is needed see Robertson, *Grammar,* pp. 254f. For other words of the first declension declined like Σατανᾶς, see βορρᾶς ("the north") and μαμωνᾶς ("Mammon").

6. Decline στέφανος.

7. Write here your own translation of I Thess. 2:17-20:

UNIT III
Interpreting the Article

LESSON 16

The Article
(το ἄρθρον)

(Dana and Mantey, pp. 135-53; Funk-Debrunner, pp. 131-45; Philip B. Harner, "Qualitative Anarthrous Predicate Nouns," *Journal of Biblical Literature,* 92 (March, 1973), pp. 75-78; Moule, pp. 106-17; Moulton, III, p. 36f, 166-84; Robertson, pp. 754ff; Robertson-Davis, pp. 274-83; Zerwick, pp. 165-92.)

There are in English two words which are designated by the term "article"—the indefinite article "a" (or "an"), and the definite article "the." In Greek there is only a definite article, ὁ, ἡ, τό. Occasionally, however, τὶς and εἷς are used with the force of an indefinite article. An example of the former is Luke 10:25—καὶ ἰδοὺ νομικός <u>τις</u> ἀνέστη ἐκπειράζων αὐτόν. . . . "And behold, a lawyer stood up testing him." An instance of the latter is Matt. 8:19—καὶ προσελθὼν <u>εἷς</u> γραμματεὺς εἶπεν αὐτῷ, Διδάσκαλε, ἀκολοήθήσω σοι ὅπου ἐὰν ἀπέρχῃ. "And a scribe having come said to him, 'Teacher, I will follow you wherever you go.'"

The basic rule in interpreting the article is as follows: Nouns which have an article are either definite or generic; nouns without an article are indefinite ("a" or "an") or qualitative.[1]

---

[1] An example of the qualitative or characterizing significance of the anarthrous noun is θεός in John 1:1. See also section on nonuse of article at end of this lesson.

Origin

ὁ, ἡ, τό was originally a demonstrative pronoun, but in the development of the language it was weakened to the force of the article.[2] It always retained something of its demonstrative force, however.

Function

Generally speaking, the article is used in Greek where the definite article would be used in English, but this rule will by no means hold true in every case. "The student must therefore pay most careful attention to its use; he must not think that it is used arbitrarily or without reason, because he finds it difficult to express its force in English" (Nunn, p. 56). "The article," adds Robertson, "is never meaningless in Greek, though it often fails to correspond with the English idiom" (p. 756).

The Greek article has been called "one of the most delicate problems in New Testament exegesis," [3] and undoubtedly its true significance has often been missed both by translators and exegetes.[4] It does more than simply make a word or an idea definite. Some words are definite enough without it (e.g., ἥλιος, sun);[5] others may be made definite by other means—for example, by the use of prepositions, pronouns,

[2] Cf. English "the," a weakened form of "this."

[3] H. A. A. Kennedy, "Recent Research in the Language of the New Testament," *Expository Times,* Vol. XII (1901), p. 343.

[4] The KJV often fails to show the significance of the article. This is largely because of the influence of the Vulgate. (In Latin there is no article, definite or indefinite.) Thus, in Matthew 5:1 τὸ ὄρος is translated "*a* mountain." It should be "*the* mountain," i.e., *the* one at hand, or the well-known mountain. In John 4:27 μετὰ γυναικὸς is translated "with *the* woman." It should be "with *a* woman." (cf. 1 Tim. 6:10, ῥίζα γὰρ πάντων τῶν κακῶν ἐστιν ἡ φιλαργυρία, "For the love of money is a root of all kinds of evil.")

[5] Cf. the English sentence, "He came to *earth*."

the genitive case, and adjectives. The distinctive force of the
Greek article is to draw attention to a word or an idea.

The New Testament exhibits the following uses of the
article:

1. *It is used generally as a pointer.* Robertson (p. 756)
defines the article as "a pointer," and this is indeed its most
basic use. (The Greek term for the article was ἄρθρον, a
word which literally denoted a "joint" [as of the body] but
was used grammatically of a "connecting word.") Robertson
(p. 756) calls the article "τὸ ὁριστικὸν ἄρθρον, the definite
article." (ὁριστικόν is from ὁρίζω, to mark off, define.) As a
pointer, the article serves:

1) To distinguish one object or person from another object
or person. Examples: ἀνέβη εἰς τὸ ὄρος, "He went up into
the mountain" (Matt. 5:1). ἱλάσθητί μοι τῷ ἁμαρτωλῷ,
"Be merciful to me, the sinner" (Luke 18:13). ὁρκίζω ὑμᾶς
τὸν Ἰησοῦν ὃν Παῦλος κηρύσσει, "I adjure you by the
Jesus whom Paul preaches" (Acts 19:13).

2) To distinguish one quality from another quality (the use
with abstract nouns).[6] Examples: ἄξιος εἶ . . .
λαβεῖν τὴν δόξην καὶ τὴν τιμὴν καὶ τὴν δύναμιν, "You
are worthy. . .to receive glory and honor and power" (Rev.
4:11). τῇ γὰρ χάριτί ἐστε σεσῳσμένοι, "For by grace you
are saved" (Eph. 2:8).[7]

---

[6] Dana and Mantey explain that abstract nouns, which express qualities,
"are ordinarily general in their character and application, and therefore
indefinite. But in Greek, when it is desired to apply the sense of an abstract
noun in some special and distinct way the article accompanies it" (p. 141).
Therefore, the article used with an abstract noun gives the quality it denotes
"a determined concrete application" (Zerwick, p. 57). Ἀλήθεια, for
example, means "truth" in general; ἡ ἀλήθεια in the New Testament
ordinarily means revealed truth, truth as it is in Christ, etc.

[7] The article with χάριτι could be interpreted as denoting previous
reference. See context of the verse.

3) To distinguish one class or one group from another class or group (generic use). Examples: ἔστω σοι ὥσπερ ὁ ἐθνικὸς καὶ ὁ τελώνης, "Let him be to you as the Gentile and the publican" (Matt. 18:17). οἱ ἄνδες, ἀγαπᾶτε τὰς γυναῖκας, "Husbands, love the (your) wives" (Eph. 5:25). Other examples may be seen in Matt. 5:3-10: οἱ πτωχοί ("the poor"), οἱ πενθοῦντες ("those who mourn"), etc.

4) To distinguish one word, phrase, clause, or sentence from other words, phrases, clauses, or sentences (bracket use). In this manner the Greek article may be used with adjectives, adverbs, pronouns, infinitives, participles, prepositional phrases, clauses, and even entire sentences. The article in such constructions gathers an expression into a single whole and points it out in a particular way. Examples: ὁ γὰρ πᾶς νόμος ἐν ἑνὶ λόγῳ πεπλήρωται, ἐν τῷ Ἀγαπήσεις τὸν πλησίον σου ὡς σεαυτόν, "For the whole law is fulfilled [summed up] in one word: 'You must love your neighbor as yourself'" (Gal. 5:14). ὁ δὲ Ἰησοὺς εἶπεν αὐτῷ, Τὸ Εἰ δύνη. . . .πάντα δυνατὰ τῷ πιστεύοντι, "But Jesus said to him, 'If you are able. . . ! All things are possible to him who believes'" (Mark 9:23).

5) To denote previous reference. The article is often used to refer to something previously mentioned in the context. The grammars sometimes call this the "anaphoric use." (The word is from a Greek word meaning "a carrying back.") Examples: πόθεν οὖν ἔχεις τὸ ὕδωρ τὸ ζῶν, "Whence then do you have the living water?" (John 4:11).

6) To identify the subject in a copulative sentence. Ordinarily the article distinguishes the subject from the predicate in a copulative sentence. Example: ὁ θεὸς ἀγάπη ἐστίν, "God is love" (1 John 4:8). When the article is used with both the subject and the predicate, the two ideas are treated as identical and interchangeable. Example: ἡ

ἁμαρτία ἐστιν *ἡ ἀνομία*, "Sin is lawlessness" or "Lawlessness is sin" (1 John 3:4).

2. *It has a special use with nouns connected by* καί. If two nouns of the same case are connected by καί and the article is used with both nouns, they refer to different persons or things. If only the first noun has the article, the second noun refers to the same person or thing referred to in the first. This is generally known as "Sharp's rule," after the grammarian Granville Sharp. Example: προσδεχόμενοι τὴν. . .ἐπιφάνειαν. . . *τοῦ* μεγάλου *θεοῦ* καὶ *Σωτῆρος* ἡμῶν Ἰησοῦ Χριστοῦ, "looking for the appearing. . .of our great God and Savior Jesus Christ" (Tit. 2:13).[8]

3. *It is sometimes restored to its original use as a pronoun.*

1) It may have the force of a demonstrative pronoun. Example: *οἱ* τοῦ Χριστοῦ, "Those who belong to the Christ" (Gal. 5:24).

2) When used with μέν and δέ it may function as an alternative pronoun. Example: ἔδωκεν *τοὺς μὲν* ἀποστόλους, *τοὺς δὲ* προφήτας, κτλ, "He gave some as apostles, others as prophets, etc." (Eph. 4:11).

3) It may function as a possessive pronoun. Example: οἱ ἄνδρες, ἀγαπᾶτε *τὰς* γυναῖκας, "Husbands, love your wives" (Eph. 5:25). πιλᾶτος. . .ἀπενίψατο *τὰς* χεῖρας, Pilate. . .washed off his hands" (Matt. 27:24).

4) It may have the force of a mild relative pronoun. Example: ἀκούσας. . .τὴν ἀγάπην *τὴν* εἰς πάντας τοὺς ἁγίους, "Having heard of. . .the love which (you have) toward all the saints" (Eph. 1:15). (Note: The English translation makes use of a relative pronoun in rendering the article following ἀγάπην, but from the Greek point of view

---

[8] There are, of course, exceptions to this rule (cf. Phil. 1:19, . . . διὰ τῆς ὑμῶν δεήσεως καὶ ἐπιχορηγίας τοῦ πνεύματος, ". . .through your supplication and the supply of the Spirit").

this article shows that the prepositional phrase εἰς . . . ἁγίους is an attributive modifier of ἀγάπην.)

Note on the Nonuse of the Article

It may be said, in light of the foregoing discussion, that the presence of the article as a rule draws attention to or *defines* more precisely the person or thing denoted by the word which it modifies. Where it is used with a phrase, clause, or sentence it calls special attention to that phrase, clause, or sentence. "The basal function of the Greek article," then, "is to point out *individual identity*" (Dana and Mantey, p. 137).

In line with this is the observation of Zerwick: ". . .with abstract nouns, which of themselves express qualities, attention is to be paid to the presence of the article, which gives to the quality a determined concrete application. . . . On the other hand, with concrete nouns it is the absence of the article which calls for attention, where, that is to say, the article was of itself to be expected or could stand in the context" (p. 57).

It is important for the student to remember that the Greek may omit the article in some instances where English requires that the definite article be used. Conversely, the Greek occasionally employs the article where English usage will not permit it. Sensitivity to both Greek and English idiom is needed.

Omission of the article, especially with words which might be expected to use it, has a *characterizing* effect on the construction. An example is John 1:1, Θεὸς ἦν ὁ λόγος. Had the article been used with Θεός, the suggestion would have been that the Word is identical with the entire essence of the Deity. As it actually stands, Θεός (without the article) is the predicate, and it is the nature and attributes of Deity that are ascribed to the Word. That is to say, it is the *nature* of the

Word, not the identity of his Person, to which attention is called by the absence of the article.

Consider also ὁ νόμος in a book such as Romans, denoting probably the written law (i.e., the Old Testament or perhaps the Mosaic law). Compare this with the anarthrous νόμος, law considered as a principle and thus wider than ὁ νόμος in application.

Interpreting the Verb

LESSON 17

General Information on the Verb

(The student should reread the section on the verb in lesson 1. Other works which may be consulted are: Dana and Mantey, pp. 154-55; Funk-Debrunner, pp. 72-76; Greenlee, "Verbs in the New Testament," *Bible Translator,* April, 1952; Robertson, pp. 303-4; Robertson-Davis, pp. 284-87.)

"Without a clear knowledge of the verb one cannot interpret a Greek sentence. Exegesis is impossible and preaching is impoverished" (Robertson-Davis, p. 286).[1]

Definition of the Verb

A verb is a word that affirms something about the subject. Usually it affirms action, but it may sometimes affirm existence or state of being. Thus, the two essential ideas in the verb are *action* (or existence or state of being) and *affirmation.* By the verb one can "make a statement, ask a question, or give a command about some person or thing" (Nunn, p. 1).

Classification of Verbs

As to form.—There are various ways of classifying verbs on the basis of form. For example, they may be classified as

---

[1] Robertson-Davis, observing that the English word "verb" is from the Latin *verbum* (meaning "word"), point out that "the verb is the word *par excellence* in the Indo-Germanic tongues and hence deserves the name" (p. 284).

thematic (ω verbs) and *athematic* (μι verbs).[2] Or they may be looked upon as *regular* and *irregular*. Regular verbs are all of those (both thematic and athematic) which form the various tenses, modes, and voices by adding the normal suffixes and prefixes or by making normal stem changes. Irregularities are of many types and varieties. Some verbs may form a given tense irregularly (e.g., καθαριῶ, Ionic future of καθαρίζω). Others may augment irregularly (e.g., εἶχον, imperfect of ἔχω) or reduplicate irregularly (e.g., ἀκήκοα, perfect of ἀκούω), etc.

From still another point of view, verbs may be viewed as either *fully developed* or *defective*. Fully developed verbs are those like λύω which developed all the tenses, voices, and modes. Defective verbs are those not found in all three voices (as, for example, deponent verbs), or not in every tense of one or more voices. Thus, ὁράω is used in the present and imperfect tenses, but ὄψομαι, an entirely different word, must serve for it in the future; and εἶδον, still another word, must be used in the aorist. The same is true of φέρω (future, οἴσω; aorist, ἤνεγκον) and many others.

As to nature.—Verbs may be classified as to their nature. Viewed in this manner, they are either *transitive* or *intransitive*. Transitive verbs, sometimes called verbs of incomplete predication, are those which require an object to complete their meaning. Such a verb, without its object, "creates a sense of suspense" (Dana-Mantey, p. 154). Intransitive verbs are verbs of complete predication; that is, they make complete sense without an object ("I stand"; "The sun shines"). Some verbs may be transitive in one context,

---

[2] The μι conjugation is confined in the New Testament mainly to five verbs: εἰμί, ἵημι, ἵστημι, δίδωμι, and τίθημι. A few verbs, such as δείκνυμι, are athematic in the present system only. Others, such as βαίνω, are athematic only in the aorist (ἔβην).

intransitive in another. Examples: "He ran a race" (transitive). "He ran" (intransitive). τυφλὸς ὢν ἄρτι βλέπω, "Although I am a blind man, now I see" (intransitive); βλέπω τοὺς ἀνσρώπους, "I see the men" (transitive). Linking verbs (sometimes called copulative or connecting) are really a special kind of intransitive verb. Such verbs do not make predications at all, but simply link the subject of a sentence with its predicate. The most common linking verbs are εἰμί, γίνομαι, and ὑπάρχω, but others are sometimes found.

Person and Number in the Verb

Person.—Ordinarily there are three persons in the Greek verb.[3] If the verb affirms action of the speaker, the first person is employed. If the action is ascribed to the one addressed, the second person is used. If the action is produced by one other than the speaker or the one addressed, the third person is employed.

Number.—In classical Greek there were three numbers (singular, dual, and plural), but in κοινή only singular and plural are found. The general rule is that a singular subject has a singular verb, a plural subject requires a plural verb. There are, however, some exceptions to this "rule of concord." Note the following examples:

1. A neuter plural subject often takes a singular verb, as in John 9:3—ἵνα φανερωθῇ τὰ ἔργα τοῦ θεοῦ, "In order that the works of God might be made manifest." However, the neuter plural sometimes employs a plural verb, particularly where the reference is to persons. Example: τὰ πρόβατα τὰ ἐμὰ τῆς φωνῆς μου ἀκούουσιν, "My sheep hear my voice" (John 10:27). ἔθνη frequently takes a plural verb, τέκνα less frequently.

---

[3] The imperative uses only the second and third persons.

2. Collective substantives, such as ὄχλος, πλῆθος, λαός, sometimes take a singular verb and sometimes a plural. Note John 6:2—*ἠκολούθει* αὐτῷ ὄχλος πολύς, ὅτι *ἐθεώρουν*..., "A great crowd was following him because they were beholding. . . ." Robertson observes that "each writer or speaker followed his bent or the humour of the moment" (p. 404).

3. It is not unusual for a compound subject to be accompanied by a singular verb. This may be variously explained. For example:

1) If the verb precedes the compound subject, it regularly agrees in number with the first member of the compound subject, as in 1 Cor. 13:13—νυνὶ δὲ *μένει* πίστις, ἐλπίς, ἀγάπη..., "And now remain faith, hope, love...." Moulton thinks this may be a type of anacoluthon; Robertson thinks "the simplest explanation . . . is that the first subject is alone in mind" (p. 405). If the verb follows the compound subject, it is nearly always put in the plural.

2) In compound constructions which stress totality, the singular verb regularly occurs regardless of its position in relation to the subject. Examples: ἕως ἂν *παρέλθῃ* ὁ οὐρανὸς καὶ ἡ γῆ..., "Until heaven and earth pass away . . ." (Matt. 5:18). ὁ ἄνεμος καὶ ἡ θάλασσα *ὑπακούει* αὐτῷ, "The wind and the sea obey him" (Mark 4:41). σὰρξ καὶ αἷμα βασιλείαν θεοῦ κληρονομῆσαι οὐ *δύναται*, "Flesh and blood are not able to inherit the kingdom of God" (1 Cor. 15:50).

LESSON 18

Voice

(Funk-Debrunner, pp. 161-66; Moulton, III, pp. 51-58; Robertson, pp. 330-43; 797-820; Zerwick, pp. 72-76.)

Transitiveness, we have seen, has to do with the relation of the verbal idea to the object. Voice tells how the action of the verb is related to the subject. There are three voices in Greek: active, middle, and passive.

Active Voice

The active is probably the oldest of the voices and is surely the one used most frequently in the New Testament. It represents the subject as producing the action or as existing. Example: Ἰωάννης ἐβάπτισεν ὕδατι, "John baptized in water" (Acts 1:5). This is what some grammarians call the *simple active*. The student should have no difficulty in recognizing or interpreting it.

The *causative active* is of two types. Sometimes the verb itself has a causative force, as in Matt. 5:45—τὸν ἥλιον αὐτοῦ ἀνατέλλει, "he causes his sun to rise." In other instances the verb itself is not causative, but the context suggests that the subject is acting through someone else. Example: ὁ πιλᾶτος τὸν Ἰησοῦν ἐμαστίγωσεν, "Pilate scourged Jesus" (John 19:1).

Passive Voice

The passive, the last of the voices to arise, represents the subject as acted upon by an outside agent, as receiving the action rather than as producing the action. It was a development from the middle, and in New Testament times overlapped somewhat the functions of that voice. As a rule, however, a clear-cut distinction may be observed. In the passive, verbs are usually intransitive, i.e., do not take an object. Example: <u>κατηγορεῖται</u> ὑπὸ τῶν Ἰουδαίων, "He is being accused by the Jews" (Acts 22:30). Some verbs, however, are transitive even in the passive. These ordinarily are verbs which in the active take two objects.[1] When they become passive, the accusative of the person becomes the subject and the accusative of the thing is retained as object. Example: κρατεῖτε τὰς παραδόσεις αὂ <u>ἐδιδάχθητε</u>, "Hold the traditions which you were taught" (2 Thess. 2:15).

Three types of passives are found: *regular* passive (subject receiving the action), *deponent* passive (subject producing the action, as though the verb were active), *reflexive* passive (subject acting on himself). Examples of the regular passive are cited in the immediately preceding paragraph. Examples of the deponent passive are: ἐβουλήθην (from βούλομαι, to wish, be willing), ἐνεθυμήθην (from ἐνθυμέομαι, to reflect on, consider), ἀπεκρίθη (from ἀποκρίνομαι, to answer). See Robertson, p. 334 for others. An example of the reflexive passive is ἀνεστράφην (from ἀναστρέφω, to turn back and forth, conduct one's self).

Middle Voice

The active voice emphasizes the action; the middle calls special attention to the subject as in some way participating in the results of the action.

The middle voice has no parallel in English and was indeed a refinement of the Greek language that was beginning to be blurred in the κοινή era. (Eventually the passive practically usurped its place.) Robertson says it is essentially the voice of personal interest, much as the dative is the case of personal

[1] See pp. 67, 68.

interest. It represents the subject as acting in relation to himself—either on himself, for himself, or by himself. What the precise relation is must be determined from the context and the significance of the verbal idea.

1. *Direct middle.*—The principal uses of the middle voice may be classed as either direct or indirect. The direct middle represents the subject as acting directly on himself and includes the *reflexive* and the *reciprocal* uses. An example of the former is ἀπήγξατο (aorist of ἀπάγχω), "he hanged himself." An example of the latter is ἐδιδάξαντο, "they were teaching one another." Note that the reciprocal middle employs a plural subject and involves an interchange of action. The reflexive middle may be either singular or plural.[2]

2. *Indirect middle.*—The indirect middle represents the subject as acting for himself or by himself. It includes those uses of the middle designated by some grammars as the *permissive* or *causative* (διὰ τί οὐχὶ μᾶλλον *ἀδικεῖσθε*, "why not rather let yourselves be wronged?"—1 Cor. 6:7; ἀναστὰς *βάπτισαι* καὶ *ἀπόλουσαι* τὰς ἁμαρτίας σου, "Arise, get yourself baptized and your sins washed away"— Acts 22:16); the *intensive*[3] (. . .αἰωνίαν λύτρωσιν *εὑράμενος*, ". . . having himself secured eternal redemption"—Heb. 9:12); and the *dynamic.* The last named is a sort of "drip-pan" category to catch all those uses of the middle that will not fit elsewhere. Verbs of mental action tend to take this form of the middle.

3. *Deponent middle.*—Some verbs are middle in form but active in meaning. Because they appear to have laid aside and

---

[2] By New Testament times the reflexive middle was disappearing. In place of it an active verb with a reflexive pronoun was increasingly used. However, the reflexive middle later experienced renewal, and in modern Greek this is almost the only use of the middle.

[3] Dana and Mantey observe: "The Greeks employed the middle where we must resort to italics" (p. 159).

lost the active voice, these verbs are often called "deponent." (The term comes from the Latin *depono,* "lay aside.") δέχομαι, "I receive," is an example of a deponent verb.[4] (Read again the discussion of "defective" verbs in Lesson 17.) Robertson, who uses the term "dynamic" instead of "deponent," explains that "the point about all dynamic [deponent] middles is that it is hard to see the distinctive force of the voice" (p. 812).

Reading Assignment

Translate the following verses, taking particular note of the voices: Matt. 1:22, 23; Luke 16:15; 1 Cor. 3:6; 16:15, 16; Gal. 6:12, 13.

---

[4] Many of the deponent verbs describe actions or states that are closely personal, in which case the sense of the middle voice is somewhat retained. (See second paragraph under "Middle Voice.") This "personal" quality of some deponents is pointed up in γεύομαι, "to taste"; ἅπτομαι, "to touch," "lay hold of"; etc.

LESSON 19

Translation and Syntax

1. Translate 1 Thess. 3:1-5.
2. Notes on the text:

Verse 1. στέγω originally meant "to cover," but came to mean "to bear up," "to endure." The latter is the meaning it has here. It is debatable whether the plural verb (εὐδοκή-σαμεν) is the editorial (literary) plural or is intended to include others with Paul in the action. All in all, it seems best to understand it as editorial. Moffatt, convinced of this interpretation, renders the verb "I," not "we." καταλειφ-θῆναι is an aor. pass. inf. of καταλείπω. A strong word meaning "to be left behind," "to be abandoned," it is used in Mark 12:19 of leaving one's loved ones at death. Its use here is an indication of the depth of Paul's feelings.

Verse 2. στηρίξαι, an aor. act. inf. of στηρίζω, and παρακαλέσαι express the purpose of Timothy's mission. The former word, originally used of putting in a support, came to be used generally of establishing, strengthening, confirming. In classical Greek it was sometimes used of putting one on a firm footing. The latter word suggests strengthening, helping, encouraging.

Verse 3. The inf. σαίνεσθαι may be construed as an epexegetical (explanatory) infinitive in loose apposition with στηρίξαι and παρακαλέσαι. (Robertson, *W.P.,* calls the infinitive epexegetical but interprets it as an accusative of general reference.) Or it may be taken as the object of παρακαλέσαι. Still again, it may be seen as an infinitive of purpose or result modifying both στηρίξαι and παρακαλέ-σαι. The word was originally used of dogs, in the sense of "to wag the tail." Then it came to mean "fawn upon," "flatter." This sense was then extended to include the connotation of "deceive," a meaning preferred by G. Milligan and Robertson. C. B. Williams employs it in his translation. But Arndt and Gingrich think "move," "disturb," or "agitate" a more suitable rendering. *Verse 4.* μέλλομεν θλίβεσθαι is a sort of periphrastic future. Such constructions with μέλλω, however, emphasize certainty as well as futurity. Some interpreters see in the present passage the notion of divine appointment. *Verse 5.* γνῶναι, an aor. act. inf. of γινώσκω, denotes purpose. μή πως introduces a clause which may be thought of as the object of an unexpressed φοβούμενος. The meaning then is, "I sent to know your faith (fearing) lest the tempter had tempted you, etc."

3. Parse the following:

1) στέγοντες (vs. 1)_____

2) παρακαλέσαι (vs. 2)_____

3) πειράζων (vs. 5)_____

4. Indicate the significance of the following:

1) πρός (vs. 4)_____

2) ὅτι clause (vs. 4)_____

3) μηκέτι instead of οὐκέτι (vs. 5)_____

_____

4) Use of an indicative verb after μή πως_____

_____

5. List the verbs of 1 Thess. 2:1-8, indicating whether each is transitive or intransitive; fully developed or defective; and classify each according to voice and voice usage.

6. Indicate the voice and usage of the following verbs:

1) εὐχαριστοῦμεν (2:13)_____

2) ἐδέξασθε (2:13)_____

3) ἐνεργεῖται (2:13)_____

4) ἐπάθετε (2:14)_____

5) ἠθελήσαμεν (2:18)_____

6) σαίνεσθαι (3:3)_____

7. Write here your own translation of 1 Thess. 3:1-5.

The Modes: Uses of the Indicative

(Burton, pp. 73-142; Funk, pp. 181-83; Moulton, III, pp. 90-93; Robertson, pp. 911-1049; Zerwick, pp. 100-109.)

Definition of mode.[1]—We have observed that the two fundamental elements in a verb are *action* (or state of being, existence) and *affirmation*. Voice and tense relate primarily to the matter of action; mode indicates the manner of the affirmation.[2] Robertson is careful to point out that mode has nothing to do with the truth or untruth of a statement. It only shows the manner in which the statement is made or how the action is conceived by the speaker or writer.

Number of modes.—There are three modes in English: indicative, subjunctive, and imperative. The indicative, by far the most frequently used, makes a statement or asks a question. (The word "indicative" suggests "stating" or "pointing out.") The subjunctive, the functions of which are more and more being taken over by the indicative,[3] is the mode of doubt, condition, wish, and the like. The imperative gives a command or makes a request.

There is not complete agreement as to the number of modes in Greek. Moulton, for example, is hesitant to call the

[1] Some grammarians prefer to use "mood," a word which suggests the speaker's *attitude of mind* when a statement is made. "Mode" suggests the *manner* in which the statement is made.

[2] Zerwick prefers to avoid the use of the terms "affirmation" and "assertion" in defining mode. "We say that the action is 'represented,' not that it is 'asserted,' or 'affirmed,' because often there is no assertion or affirmation, e.g. in questions, exhortations, etc." (p. 100).

[3] In English, it has been estimated that 98% of the verbs are put in the indicative mode.

indicative a mode, preferring to look upon it as the standard verb and to use the term mode only of the variations from the indicative. Others, like Robertson and Davis, consider the indicative "the chief mode and the others 'side modes' " *(Short Grammar,* p. 306). Robert W. Funk, on the other hand, includes both the infinitive and the participle among the modes. We follow Robertson and Davis, however, at this point. They contend that the infinitive and the participle are "obviously not modes, since they are without personal endings or mode suffixes . . . That leaves four modes in the Greek (indicative, subjunctive, optative, imperative)" *(Short Grammar,* p. 306).

Points of view.—There are really only two viewpoints represented by the modes: the action may be considered as real (actual), or the action may be considered as potential (possible). The indicative covers the former; the latter embraces the subjunctive, optative, and imperative.

The Indicative

The indicative is the mode of fact, or rather of statement presented as fact. Robertson calls it the mode of definite assertion and explains that "it is the normal mode to use when there is no special reason for employing another mode" *(Grammar,* p. 915). Dana and Mantey describe it as "the mood of certainty" (p. 168). By far the most frequently used, the indicative states the verbal idea from the point of view of reality. However, it "does not guarantee the reality of the thing. In the nature of the case only the statement is under discussion" (Robertson, p. 915). Zerwick comments: "What matters is how the act is conceived by the speaker, not its objective nature" (p. 100). The New Testament exhibits the following uses of the indicative:

Primary Uses

The indicative is used mainly to make a statement or to ask a simple question. The former is called the *declarative* indicative, the latter the *interrogative* indicative. There is no essential difference between them. One states a simple fact (or states a thing as fact); the other asks a question which may be answered factually. Compare these examples: Declarative, ὁ λόγος σὰρξ ἐγένετο, "The word became flesh" (John 1:14). Interrogative, πιστεύεις τοῦτο, "Do you believe this?" (John 11:26).

Special Uses

Possibly at the beginning the indicative was used "to express all the various moods or tones of the speaker" (Robertson, p. 912), and to some extent it retained "all the functions of all the modes" (Robertson, p. 918). The New Testament uses the indicative to express the following ideas. (Note that most of them may be expressed in other modes.)

1. *Command.*—The *future* indicative is sometimes used to express a command. Dana and Mantey call this the "cohortative" indicative. Example: καλέσεις τὸ ὄνομα αὐτοῦ Ἰησοῦν, "You must call his name Jesus" (Matt. 1:21).

2. *Condition.*—The indicative is used in the protasis of both first and second class conditional sentences. Examples: εἴ τις ἔχει ὦτα ἀκούειν ἀκουέτω, "If anyone has ears to hear, let him hear" (Mark 4:23). οὗτος εἰ ἦν προφήτης, ἐγίνωσκεν ἂν τίς καὶ τοταπὴ ἡ γυνὴ, "If this man were a prophet, he would have known who and what sort of woman this is" (Luke 7:39). κύριε, εἰ ἦς ὧδε οὐκ ἂν μου ἀπέθανεν ὁ ἀδελφός, "Lord, if you had been here, my brother would not have died" (John 11:32). (Note that in the second class condition both protasis and apodosis employ the indicative.)

3. *Wish or impulse.*—The imperfect indicative may be

used in expressing a wish or an impulse hesitantly or politely, or to express a wish that is known to be unattainable. The statement is put into past time, but present time is contemplated. Examples: *ηὐχόμην* ἀνάθεμα εἶναι, "I could wish to be accursed" (Rom. 9:3). *ἐβουλόμην* αὐτὸς τοῦ ἀνθρώπου ἀκοῦσαι, "I myself have been rather wanting to hear the man" (Acts 25:22).

4. *Obligation, necessity, propriety.*—The secondary tenses of the indicative may be used in expressions of obligation, necessity, or propriety. The suggestion ordinarily is that the obligation, necessity, etc. has not been lived up to . Example: οὕς *ἔδει* ἐπὶ σοῦ παρεῖναι, "Who ought to be here before you" (Acts 24:19).

Reading Assignment

Translate the following verses, giving special attention to the indicative verbs: Matt. 25:27; Mark 1:24; John 1:12-14; Gal. 4:20; Phil. 1:3; 1 Pet. 1:16.

The Subjunctive and the Optative Modes

(Burton, pp. 74-80; Funk, pp. 183-95; Moulton, III, pp. 93-133; Robertson, pp. 924-40; Zerwick, pp. 354-58.)

The Subjunctive

The subjunctive mode is used for doubtful, hesitating assertions (Robertson, p. 927). Nunn says it "expresses a thought [a conception of the mind] or a wish [something planned or desired] rather than a fact" (*Short Syntax,* p. 61). Since the subjunctive is a potential mode, it always denotes an action which is future. In this respect, it is closely related to the future indicative.

Uses in Principal (Independent) Clauses

Its name suggests that the subjunctive is confined to dependent (subjoined) clauses, but this is not the case. It is used widely in both independent clauses and dependent clauses.

Four uses of the subjunctive as a main verb in independent clauses may be noted:

1. *Exhortation.*—The subjunctive in independent clauses may be hortatory. This is the use of the first person plural by a speaker or writer to exhort others to join with him in an action. Robertson calls this "volitive." Example: ἀγαπητοί, *ἀγαπῶμεν* ἀλλήλους, "Beloved, let us keep on loving one another" (1 John 4:7).

2. *Deliberation.*—The subjunctive in independent clauses may be deliberative. This use of the subjunctive expresses perplexity on the part of the speaker. It asks a question which

represents a *doubtful state of mind* or which is used only as a *rhetorical device.* Example: τί φάγωμεν, "What shall we eat?" (Matt. 6:31).

3. *Prohibition.*—The subjunctive in independent clauses is sometimes used to express prohibition. This construction always employs the aorist tense; generally the second person is used, though occasionally the third person occurs. (Note: The second person of the aorist imperative is never used in prohibition.) Examples: μὴ μεριμνήσητε, "Don't ever be anxious" (Matt. 6:31). μή τις αὐτὸν ἐξουθενήσῃ, "Let no one despise him" (1 Cor. 16:11).[1]

4. *Strong denial.*—The subjunctive in an independent clause may be used to express strong denial. (Dana and Mantey call this "emphatic negation.") The subjunctive so used occurs with οὐ μή and the aorist tense.[2] It is the strongest way to make a negative statement of a future occurrence. Example: οὐ μὴ ἀπόλωνται, "They shall never perish" (John 10:28).

Uses in Subordinate (Dependent) Clauses

In certain types of dependent clauses the subjunctive is the normal mode to use. These are *purpose clauses* (generally introduced by ἵνα or ὅπως); *indefinite temporal clauses* (introduced by ἕως ἄν, ὅταν, ἐπάν, ἄχρι, ἄχρι οὗ, μέχρι, etc.); *indefinite relative clauses* (introduced by ὅς ἄν, etc.); *third class conditional clauses* (usually introduced by ἐάν); *substantive clauses* after ἵνα (subject, object, appositive, etc.); and result clauses after ἵνα. Examples: purpose—

---

[1] There are a few passages in the New Testament in which a subjunctive verb with ἵνα appears to have imperatival force (e.g. Mark 5:23; 2 Cor. 8:7; Eph. 5:33). It is possible, however, that an unexpressed verb should be understood with the ἵνα construction.

[2] Occasionally οὐ μή with a future indicative expresses strong denial.

ταῦτα γράφω ὑμῖν ἵνα μὴ *ἁμάρτητε,* "These things I am writing to you in order that you may not sin" (1 John 2:1); indefinite temporal—σὺ δὲ *ὅταν προσεύχῃ,* εἴσελθε . . . , "And whenever you pray, enter . . . " (Matt. 6:6); indefinite relative—*ὃς ἄν ἐπικαλέσηται* τὸ ὄνομα κυρίου σωθήσεται, "Whoever calls upon the name of the Lord will be saved" (Rom. 10:13); condition—ἐὰν *ὁμολογήσῃς* . . . κύριον Ἰησοῦν, καὶ *πιστεύσῃς* . . . σωθήσῃ, "If you confess. . . Jesus as Lord, and believe . . . you will be saved" (Rom. 10:10); substantive—καὶ τοῦτο προσεύχομαι, ἵνα ἡ ἀγάπη ὑμῶν . . . *περισσεύῃ,* "And this I pray, that your love . . . may go on abounding" (Phil. 1:9); result—λέγω οὖν, μὴ ἔπταισαν ἵνα *πέσωσιν;* "I say then, did they stumble so that they fell?" (Rom. 11:11).

The Optative

The subjunctive is the mode of probability; the optative is the mode of possibility. The two do not differ radically.

The optative is "a sort of weaker subjunctive" (Robertson, p. 936), and like the subjunctive expresses a doubtful or contingent statement. In the *Koine* period it was on the wane, and is used in the New Testament only sixty-seven times—and only in the present and aorist tenses.

Uses of the Optative

The most frequent uses of the optative are as follows:

1. *In the expression of a wish.*—The optative may be used to express a wish. There are approximately thirty-eight of these in the New Testament (Moulton, *Prolegomena,* pp. 194f), of which fifteen are instances of μὴ γένοιτο, "May it not be" or, as the King James Version translates it, "God forbid!" Another example: χάρις ὑμῖν καὶ εἰρήνη *πληθυν-*

θείη, "May grace and peace be multiplied to you" (1 Pet. 1:2).

2. *In conditional sentences.*—The optative was used in both the protasis and apodosis of conditions of the fourth class. (Note: No example of this condition complete in both protasis and apodosis occurs in the New Testament.) Example: εἰ καὶ πάσχοιτε διὰ δικαιοσύνην, μακάριοι, "Even if you should suffer on account of righteousness, happy are you" (1 Pet. 3:14).

3. *In indirect rhetorical questions.*—When an especially doubtful state of mind is implied, indirect rhetorical questions employ the optative. Example: διελογίζετο ποταπὸς εἴη ὁ ἀσπασμὸς οὗτος, "She was wondering what kind of greeting this might be" (Luke 1:29). (Arndt, *Commentary*, p. 53, says the use of the optative after a secondary tense is here an instance of Luke's "fine feeling for literary niceties.")

Reading Assignment

Translate the following passages, giving special attention to the subjunctive and optative constructions: Matt. 5:20; Mark 5:6-7; Rom. 6:1-2; Phil. 1:9; Heb. 3:7-8; 4:16.

LESSON 22

The Imperative Mode

(W. F. Bakker, *The Greek Imperative;* Burton, pp. 80-81; Funk, pp. 195-96; Moulton, I, pp. 171-84; Robertson, pp. 941-50.)

The imperative is by no means confined to commands, but it is essentially the mode of "commanding statement" (Robertson, p. 928). Moulton observes that imperatives are "normal in royal edicts, in letters to inferiors, and among equals when the tone is urgent, or the writer indisposed to multiply words" (I, p. 173). Dana and Mantey explain that the imperative "expresses neither probability nor possibility, but only intention, and is, therefore, the further removed from reality" (p. 174).

The Uses of the Imperative

1. *Command.*—Though there are other ways of doing this,[1] the imperative is the normal mode to use in the assertion of one's will over another. Example: πάντοτε *χαίρετε,* "Rejoice always" (1 Thess. 5:16); *γίνεσθε* ποιηταὶ λόγου, "Become doers of the word" (James 1:22).

2. *Prohibition.*[2]—The present imperative with μή is

[1] We have already seen that the future indicative may have imperatival force and that the aorist subjunctive may be used to express negative commands. Later we will observe that both the infinitive and the participle may express commands. It should be remembered that the imperative was the last of the modes to be developed, and some of the methods of making commands before there was an imperative continued to be used after its appearance.

[2] A prohibition really is only a negative command, and so the imperative of prohibition is not essentially different from the imperative of command.

frequently used to express a prohibition. (Prohibitions in the aorist tense, especially in the second person, are normally expressed by the subjunctive mode. See Lesson 21.) A present imperative with μή forbids the continuance of an act already in progress. Thus μὴ φοβοῦ, "Stop being afraid" (Rev. 1:17); ἀδελφοί μου, μὴ *ὀμνύετε*, "My brothers, swear not" (James 5:12). The aorist subjunctive with μή differs from the present imperative in that it forbids an act before it has begun; i.e., it commands never to do a thing. Example: *μηδένα* κατὰ τὴν ὁδὸν *ἀσπάσησθε*, "Greet nobody along the way" (Luke 10:4).

3. *Entreaty.*—Sometimes the tone of command in the imperative "is softened to pleading" (Robertson, p. 947). Examples are: *βοήθησον* ἡμῖν, "Help us!" (Mark 9:22). *πρόσθες* ἡμῖν πίστιν, "Increase our faith" (Luke 17:5).

4. *Permission.*—Sometimes the command of the imperative is in compliance with the desire or inclination of the person addressed. Thus the emphasis is on granting a permission (or giving consent) rather than on issuing a command. Example: *καθεύδετε* τὸ λοιπὸν καὶ *ἀναπαύεσθε*, "Sleep on now, and refresh yourselves" (Matt. 26:45); *ὀργίζεσθε* καὶ μὴ ἁμαρτάνετε, "You may be angry, but do not sin" (Eph. 4:26); εἰ δὲ ὁ ἄπιστος χωρίζεται, *χωριζέσθω*, "But if the unbeliever departs, let him depart" (1 Cor. 7:15).

5. *Concession or condition.*—In certain contexts the imperative may be the equivalent of a conditional or concessive clause. This use of the imperative, like the imperative of permission, suggests an inclination on the part of the persons addressed to do the thing mentioned. Example: λύσατε τὸν ναὸν τοῦτον [= ἐὰν καὶ λύσητε τὸν ναὸν τοῦτον] καὶ ἐν τρισὶν ἡμέραις ἐγερῶ αὐτόν,

"Destroy this temple [= even if you destroy this temple], and in three days I will raise it" (John 2:19).

Reading Assignment

Translate Matt. 6:7-13, noting especially the subjunctive and imperative verbs.

LESSON 23

Translation and Syntax

1. Translate 1 Thess. 3:6-13.
2. Notes on the text:

Verse 6. ἄρτι suggests that this epistle was written shortly after Timothy reached Paul with his report of the situation at Thessalonica. εὐαγγελισαμένου, part of a genitive absolute construction, is used only here in the New Testament of announcing good news other than that of the saving work of God in Christ. Its use here suggests the joy with which Paul received the news about the Thessalonians. ἐπιποθοῦντες agrees in case and number with the unexpressed subject of ἔχετε.

Verse 7. Observe the two locatives with ἐπί; the former in the sense of "over" or "about," the other in the sense of "in." ἀνάγκη, which basically means "necessity," here speaks of physical necessity. Some of the versions render it "distress." The root meaning of θλίψις is "pressure."

Verse 8. ζῶμεν is a pres. act. ind. of ζάω. Note the ῶ, a contraction of α and ο. Note the emphatic ὑμεῖς. στήκω is a late verb derived from ἕστηκα (perf. of ἵστημι). It probably conveys the idea of standing firm.

Verse 9. ἀνταποδοῦναι is an aor. act. inf. of ἀνταποδίδωμι.

Verse 10. ὑπερεκπερισσοῦ is a double compound adverb, used in the New Testament only here, in Eph. 3:20, and in 1 Thess. 5:13. δέομαι denotes prayer arising from a sense of need. ἰδεῖν is an infinitive expressing purpose. καταρτίσαι is an aorist inf. of καταρτίζω, to mend, perfect.

Verse 11. This verse introduces a prayer which continues

109

through verse 13. κατευθύναι is an aor. act. opt. of κατευθύνω. Except for accent, the form is the same as the aor. act. inf. The root meaning of the word is "to make a straight path," but here it has the general sense of "direct."

Verse 12. δέ should probably be interpreted as having adversative ("but") force here. πλεονάσαι and περισσεύσαι are also aor. act. opts., from πλεονάζω and περισσεύω respectively. The two words are practically synonymous in meaning and the use of both, rather than just one, makes the expression emphatic.

Verse 13. Observe the predicate position of ἀμέμπτους. πάντων τῶν ἀγίων αὐτοῦ would ordinarily refer to God's redeemed people, but here the expression may be a reference to all those "holy ones" who accompany our Lord when he returns to earth, whether they are angels or redeemed men who already live in the realm of glory.

   3. Give the case syntax of the following:

     1) ἐλθόντος Τιμοθέου (vs. 6)_____

     2) ἡμῶν (vs. 6)_____

     3) τοῦτο (vs. 7)_____

     4) θεῷ (vs. 9)_____

     5) νυκτός (vs. 10)_____

     6) αὐτός (vs. 11)_____

     7) ἀλλήλους (vs. 12)_____

   4. Explain the following constructions:

     1) ἐάν . . . στήκετε instead of ἐάν . . . στήκητε (vs.

        8)._____

2) ἡμέρας instead of ἡμέραν (vs. 10)._____

_____

_____

3) The article in ὁ . . . πατήρ (vs. 11). _____

_____

4) The plural subject and singular verb of verse

11._____

5) The usage of these optatives:

κατευθύναι (vs. 11)_____

πλεονάσαι (vs. 11)_____

περισσεύσαι (vs. 11)_____

6) The usage of καταρτίσαι (vs. 10) and στηρίξαι (vs.

13). Consult a commentary if necessary._____

_____

5. Write out here your own translation of 1 Thess. 3:6-13.

LESSON 24

Translation and Syntax

1. Translate 1 Thess. 4:1-6.
2. Notes on the text:

Verse 1. λοιπὸν οὖν marks a transition and introduces an exhortation to godly conduct. λοιπόν, an accusative of reference, may be literally rendered "with reference to the rest." Robertson calls it "a colloquial expression pointing towards the end" (*W.P.* Vol. IV, p. 28). ἐρωτῶμεγ and παρακαλοῦμεν are practically synonymous here. The use of the two words gives a certain fullness and intensity. The article τό goes with the entire indirect question introduced by πῶς. δεῖ, an impersonal verb, indicates that upright conduct is not optional for the Christian but is a matter of necessity. ἵνα ... περισσεύητε is the object of ἐρωτῶμεν καὶ παρακαλοῦμεν. (ἵνα is repeated immediately before περισσεύητε simply to resume the thought begun earlier in the verse by the first ἵνα.)

Verse 2. τίνας, an interrogative pronoun, functions here with adjectival force. See Arndt and Gingrich, meaning 2. παραγγελίας is not common in Christian writings, although it does appear in 1 Tim. 1:5, 18, with a sense somewhat like its meaning here. The term is ordinarily used for instructions or commands, and occurs frequently in the papyri, especially in reference to military orders (cf. Acts 5:28; 16:24). Morris *(NICNT)* calls it "a word with a ring of authority." The use of διά in this passage is somewhat unusual. We might have expected ἐν. Lightfoot understands the phrase in the text to mean something like "prompted by the Lord."

Verses 3-8 define the rigid sexual purity which the Lord demands. Note that θέλημα (vs. 3) does not have an article;

thus, sexual purity is represented as only a part, not the whole, of God's will for man. The will of God is defined by the word ἁγιασμός. Then it is more specifically defined by two epexegetical (explanatory) infinitives: ἀπέχεσθαι (vs. 3) and εἰδέναι (vs. 4). It is possible that ὑπερβαίνειν (vs. 6) and πλεονεκτεῖν (vs. 6) should be interpreted in the same way, i.e., as coordinate with ἀπέχεσθαι and εἰδέναι.

Verse 4. σκεῦος is interpreted by some to mean wife and by others to be a reference to the body. The meaning then is either "to possess (acquire) his own wife" or "to possess his own body." (Check Arndt and Gingrich on the meaning of κτάομαι, and note that in the perfect it has present meaning and is to be translated "possess.") Robertson *(W.P.)* and Morris *(NICNT),* along with the early Greek commentators, prefer the former. Frame takes εἰδέναι to mean something like "respect," "appreciate the worth of" (cf. 5:12). εἰδέναι is a perf. act. inf. of οἶδα. κτᾶσθαι is a pres. mid. inf. of κτάομαι.

Verse 5. ἐπιθυμία (desire) denotes strong desire of any kind, though generally in the New Testament it has a bad connotation. πάθος, which denotes an overmastering feeling, is always used in a bad sense.

Verse 6. ὑπερβαίνειν and πλεονεκτεῖν represent promiscuity as "an act of injustice to someone other than the two parties concerned" (Morris, *NICNT).* τὸ μή has given interpreters great difficulty. The construction may indicate that the two infinitives with which it is employed have the force of final clauses. If so, the infinitives express a twofold purpose of ἀπέχεσθαι (vs. 3) and εἰδέναι (vs. 4).

3. Give the case and syntax of the following:

1) ἁγιασμός (vs. 3)_____

2) ὑμᾶς (vs. 3)_____

3) ἀδελφόν (vs. 6)_____

4. Select the indicatives of verses 1-2 and classify each according to usage.

5. Using the following chart, list the infinitives of 4:1-6 and give the information requested. (Refer to a commentary such as Robertson's *Word Pictures* or Frame's work in *The International Critical Commentary,* if necessary; you may also look ahead to Lesson 42.)

Verse	Infinitive	Word Related to	Function

6. Write out here your own translation of 1 Thess. 4:1-6.

LESSON 25

Translation and Syntax

1. Translate 1 Thess. 4:7-12.
2. Notes on the text:

Verse 7. ἐπί probably denotes purpose: "for," "for the purpose of" (Cf. Dana and Mantey, p. 106). ἐν ἁγιασμῷ is understood by Lightfoot to be an abbreviation for ὥστε εἶναι ἐν ἁγιασμῷ.

Verse 8. τοιγαροῦν is a triple compound particle, used in the New Testament only here and Heb. 12:1. It is perhaps stronger than διὰ τοῦτο, διό or ὥστε. Note the three reasons for moral purity given in verse 6b-8.

Verse 9. γράφειν is an infinitival modifier of χρείαν, thus, "a to-write-to-you kind of need." An unexpressed ἡμᾶς (or τινα) is to be understood as the adverbial accusative of reference used with γράφειν. Some interpreters see the εἰς τὸ ἀγαπᾶν as an epexegetic (explanatory) infinitive. It could be construed, however, as expressing purpose. This interpretation is perhaps to be preferred.

3. Give the syntax of the following:

1) αὐτοί (vs. 9)_____

2. αὐτό (vs. 10)_____

3) ἀδελφούς (vs. 10)_____

4) χερσίν (vs.11)_____

5) μηδενός (vs. 12)_____

4. List the subjunctives of this passage and give the use of each.

5. List the infinitives of the passage, indicating the word to which each is related.

6. Write out here your own translation of 1 Thess. 4:7-12.

LESSON 26

Translation and Syntax

1. Translate 1 Thess. 4:13-18.

2. Notes on the text:

The opening verse introduces one of the more important doctrinal sections of 1 Thessalonians, dealing with two matters that were of particular concern to the Thessalonians: 1) the fate of believers who die before the Lord's return (4:13-18) and 2) the time of the Lord's return (5:1-11). Milligan points out that the two sections, 4:13-18 and 5:1-11, are closely parallel. Each contains a question, 4:13 and 5:1; each records an answer, 4:14-17 and 5:2-10; and each concludes with a practical exhortation, 4:18 and 5:11.

Verses 13, 14. οὐ θέλομεν δὲ ὑμᾶς ἀγνοεῖν is a formula used by Paul to arrest the attention of his readers and direct their thoughts to something new (cf. Rom. 1:13; 11:25; 1 Cor. 10:1; 12:1; 2 Cor. 1:8). Note the tenses of κοιμωμένων (present) and κοιμηθέντας (aorist). The present tense here has iterative force, "falling asleep from time to time." Morris thinks the perfect tense would ordinarily have been expected, but the use of the present "points forward to the future awakening more definitely than would the perfect" *(NICNT).* The aorist may be rendered, "those who have fallen asleep." In the active κοιμάω has a causative meaning, to lull or put to sleep. In the middle and passive it means to sleep.

Verse 15. ἐν λόγῳ may refer to a direct revelation of the Lord (cf. 1 Cor. 11:23). If during his earthly ministry Jesus gave specific instructions at this point, they have not been preserved.

The first person ἡμεῖς may seem to imply that the apostle

120

expected to be alive when the Lord returned. Calvin suggests that the first person is employed simply to keep the Thessalonians alert. Robertson thinks it was the natural way for Paul to write, for "He was alive, not dead, when he wrote." Morris agrees with Lightfoot's paraphrase, "When I say 'we,' I mean those who are living, those who survive to that day."

Verse 16. κελεύσματι is a term often used with reference to a military order. πρῶτον indicates that the dead will not only participate in the parousia, they will arise before those alive are changed.

Verses 17, 18. ἅμα appears here to be an adverbial (improper) preposition used pleonastically with σύν (cf. Arndt and Gingrich, meaning 2.). Frame gives ἅμα adverbial force, "simultaneously." ἔπειτα introduces an action which occurs immediately following that defined by the πρῶτον (vs. 16).

3. Select the finite verbs of this passage and classify the mode of each according to its usage.

4. Give the case syntax of the following:

     1) ἀδελφοί (vs. 13)_____

     2) ὑμᾶς (vs. 13)_____

     3) αὐτῷ (vs. 14)_____

     4) αὐτός (vs. 16)_____

     5) αὐτοῖς (vs. 17)_____

     6) νεφέλαις (vs. 17)_____

     7) ἀπάντησιν (vs. 17)_____

5. Explain the syntax of the following clauses:

     1) ἵνα (vs. 13)_____

     2) εἰ (vs. 14)_____

     3) ὅτι (vs. 14)_____

     4) οὕτως (vs. 14)_____

     5) ὅτι (vs. 15)_____

     6) οὕτως (vs. 17)_____

6. Explain the significance of the tense of λυπῆσθε (vs. 13)._____

---

7. See Arndt and Gingrich, p. 69, for explanation of the voice of ἀναστήσονται (vs. 16).

8. Write out here your own translation of 1 Thess. 4:13-18.

LESSON 27

Translation and Syntax

1. Translate 1 Thess. 5:1-11.
2. Notes on the text:

Verse 1. χρόνων denotes time in its chronological aspect, while καιρῶν defines time qualitatively; the former refers to chronological epochs, the latter to critical events (Morris). Note that γράφεσθαι modifies χρείαν; thus, the meaning is a "to-be-written-to-you kind of need" (cf. note on 4:9). τι is to be supplied as the accusative of reference with γράφεσθαι.

Verse 2. The absence of articles with ἡμέρα shows the phrase had become a fixed formula, a sort of technical term. ἔρχεται is a futuristic present, which lends vividness to the idea of the verb. Frame, however, understands this to be a gnomic present, expressing a general or timeless truth. See Lesson 30.

Verse 3. The absence of a connecting particle at the beginning of verse 3 indicates the close connection of this verse with what precedes. Although the subject of λέγωσιν is undefined, the reference is obviously to unbelievers. The plural is sometimes used when an idea is expressed indefinitely. ἀσφάλεια, used in the New Testament only here and in Luke 1:4 and Acts 5:23, here has the meaning of safety, security. ὄλεθρος, destruction, is built on the root of ὄλλυμι, to destroy. τῇ ἐν γαστρὶ ἐχούσῃ is an idiom equivalent to "the pregnant woman."

Verse 5. "Sons of" is a Semitic idiom used to characterize or describe. "Sons of light," then, are persons whose distinguishing trait is light.

Verse 6. ἄρα οὖν is a strong expression of inference used here to introduce "an inescapable conclusion" (Morris, *TNTC*). Such words are always important to interpretation.

γρηγορῶμεν and νήφωμεν are similar in meaning, but the former is a reference to mental alertness while νήφωμεν has a moral connotation.

Verse 7. μεθύσκω has causative force, to cause to become intoxicated. It is used in the New Testament only in the passive, with the meaning to get drunk, to be drunk.

Verse 8. ὄντες is a causal participle, thus giving the ground or basis of action contained in the main verb.

Verse 10. Note the use of εἴτε (rather than ἐάντε) to introduce a third class condition. The two particles give "alternative" conditions.

Verse 11. εἷς is a nominative in partitive apposition with the subject of οἰκοδομεῖτε. τὸν ἕνα is accusative in partitive apposition with the unexpressed object of οἰκοδομεῖτε.

3. Numerous subjunctives appear in 1 Thess. 5:1-11. List them and classify each according to its usage.

4. Give the case syntax of the following:

1) νυκτί (vs. 2)_____

2) Εἰρήνη (vs. 3)_____

3) ὠδίν (vs. 3)_____

4) νυκτός (vs. 7)_____

5) πίστεως (vs. 8)_____

6) περικεφαλαίαν (vs. 8)_____

7) αὐτῷ (vs. 10)_____

8) εἷς (vs. 11)_____

5. Write out here your own translation of 1 Thess. 5:1-11.

Translation and Syntax

1. Translate 1 Thess. 5:12-28.
2. Notes on the text:

Verses 12, 13. These verses, addressed to the whole membership, urge respect and esteem for church leaders. The common article used with κοπιῶντας, προϊσταμένους and νουθετοῦντας (vs. 12) indicates that the three participles are describing three functions of one group or class of persons. (See "Sharp's rule" for the article, Lesson 16.) The reference is probably to elders (i.e., bishops or pastors), because only they would exercise the triple function expressed by the participles.

The two infinitives (εἰδέναι . . . καὶ ἡγεῖσθαι) are dependent on ἐρωτῶμεν. The first, in this context, means something like "respect," "appreciate the worth of"; the second, which is very similar in meaning, perhaps conveys more of the idea of right feeling.

Verse 14. Like the remainder of this passage, verse 14 is for the church at large; but Paul seems to have the leaders of the church especially in mind.

Verse 15. μή, introducing an object clause (or a negative purpose clause) after ὁρᾶτε, has conjunctive force. It sometimes serves in this capacity after verbs of fearing, warning, and caution (Dana and Mantey, p. 294; Robertson, pp. 430, 995, 1169).

Verse 18. τοῦτο γὰρ θέλημα κτλ is understood by most interpreters to go with all three commands of verses 16-18. Denney calls the three imperatives of these verses "the standing orders" of the church (*Expositor's Bible*, p. 217).

127

Observe the absence of the article with θέλημα, and compare the note on 1 Thess. 4:3.

Verse 21. The prepositional prefix in κατέχετε is perfective. That is to say, it intensifies the idea of the verb with which it is compounded. See Lesson 1 on the preposition.

Verse 22. εἶδος may be used in two different ways: it may be used of outward appearance or form (e.g., bodily *form,* Luke 3:22; *appearance* of the face, Luke 9:29); or it may be used in the sense of sort, species, or kind. The latter is the meaning which the word has in the present passage—"every *kind* of evil." (The idea of "semblance" as opposed to reality, a meaning popularly assigned to the KJV translation, is not attested elsewhere. Cf. NAB.)

Verse 23. ὁλοτελεῖς (pl.) and ὁλόκληρον (sing.) are both predicate adjectives, the former in the accusative case and the latter in the nominative. The two words are virtually synonymous in meaning. ὁλοτελεῖς, a predicate accusative, is translated here by Lightfoot as follows: "may He sanctify you so that ye be entire." Robertson takes it to mean "the whole of each of you, every part of each of you" *(W.P.).* Others (e.g. Luther, Frame) understand it as having adverbial force, conveying the sense of through and through. ὁλόκληρον, which means "complete in all its parts, undamaged," is also placed in the predicate position. The singular adjective and the singular verb, used with a compound subject, perhaps show that Paul was thinking of man as "an undivided whole" (Frame).

3. Select the finite verbs of verses 12-15 and classify each mode according to its usage.

4. Indicate the usage of the following infinitives:

1) εἰδέναι (vs. 12)_____

2) ἡγεῖσθαι (vs. 13)_____

5. Give the case and syntax of these substantives:

1) ὑμῖν (vs. 12)_____

2) ὑμῶν (vs. 12)_____

3) ἀτάκτους (vs. 14)——————————

4) ἀσθενῶν (vs. 14)——————————

5) κακοῦ (vs. 15)——————————

6) ἀλλήλους (vs. 15)——————————

7) ὑμᾶς (vs. 18)——————————

8) αὐτός (vs. 23)——————————

9) πιστός (vs. 24) ——————————

10) ὑμᾶς (vs. 27)——————————

11) κύριον (vs. 27)——————————

12) ἐπιστολήν (vs. 27)——————————

13) ἀδελφοῖς (vs. 27)——————————

6. List the imperatives of verses 16-28 and give the usage of each.

7. ἀγιάσαι (vs. 23) and τηρηθείη (vs. 23) are optatives.

Indicate their usage._____

8. Write out here your own translation of 1 Thess. 5:12-28.

LESSON 29

Tense

(Chamberlain, pp. 67-69; Funk-Debrunner, pp. 166-67; Moulton, I, pp. 109-19; III, pp. 59, 60; Robertson, pp. 343-45, 821-28; Zerwick, pp. 77, 78.)

Robertson observes that "probably nothing connected with syntax is so imperfectly understood by the average student as tense" (p. 821). Chamberlain, in line with this, points out that "most of these errors have grown out of the habit of trying to equate the Greek tenses with Latin, English or German tenses" (p. 70).

Classification of the Tenses

Greek tenses are classified in the indicative mode as *primary* (or principal) and *secondary* (or historical). The primary tenses (present, future, perfect, and future perfect) denote present and future time. The secondary tenses (imperfect, aorist, pluperfect) denote past time. The augment used with the secondary tenses is an attempt to bring out this idea of past time.

Action in the Tenses

The tenses may express two relations. They may designate the *time* of an action as past, present, or future; they may also designate the *state* or *progress* of the action as incomplete, completed, or undefined. The time element appears directly only in the indicative mode. In other modes, as well as in the infinitive and the participle, the time element is only relative if it appears at all. The state or progress of the action is a

132

matter of primary importance in all the modes and in the infinitive and the participle.

As stated above, there are three kinds[1] of action exhibited by Greek tenses. These may be defined as follows:

1) Incomplete or linear. This represents the action as *going on* (in progress) and may be represented by a line (———).

2) Completed or perfected. This views the action as a *finished product* and emphasizes the existence of results growing out of the completed act. It may be represented by a dot followed by a line (.———).

3) Undefined or punctiliar. This represents the action as simply an *occurrence* and may be represented by a dot (.). It makes no reference to the continuity or completeness of the action.

Each of these kinds of action may be expressed in the *indicative mode* in either past, present, or future time. The following diagram illustrates this.

	Present time	Past time	Future time
Linear	Pres. tense	Imperf. tense	Fut. tense
Perfected	Perf. tense	Pluperf. tense	Fut. perf. tense
Punctiliar	(Pres. tense)[2]	Aorist tense	Fut. tense

Compare the following sentences as examples of the above:

Linear action:　　I am writing a book. (Present)
　　　　　　　　　I was writing a book. (Past)
　　　　　　　　　I will be writing a book. (Future)

Perfected action:　I have written a book. (Present)
　　　　　　　　　I had written a book. (Past)
　　　　　　　　　I will have written a book. (Future)

[1] Some grammars refer to this as "aspects" of the action.
[2] This is a specialized use of the present indicative.

Punctiliar action:　　I write a book. (Present)

I wrote a book. (Past)

I will write a book. (Future)

Aktionsart of Greek Verbs

Aktionsart, a German word meaning "kind of action," is employed by modern grammarians to refer to the idea of kind of action as it is expressed by the Greek verb roots. Students often overlook the fact that kind of action was at first expressed altogether by the verb roots. Only gradually did the tenses come to be used to denote this idea.

Davis states that "there were originally two verb-types, the one denoting durative or linear action, the other momentary, or punctiliar action" (p. 123).[3] For some time the present tense was confined to durative stems and the aorist was limited to punctiliar stems. Indeed, the linear idea was so persistent in some roots that they were never used in the aorist, and a good synonym from a punctiliar root made it unnecessary. This explains the existence of many so-called irregular verbs. For example, the verb ἐσθίω ("I am eating") expressed the linear idea, while the root φαγ- expressed the idea from the punctiliar point of view. Consequently, ἔφαγον is used in the aorist, and ἐσθίω is used in the present and imperfect.

Eventually, however, the aorist came to be made on durative stems and the present was formed on punctiliar stems. When this happened, the present tense imposed a durative idea on a punctiliar verb root, and the aorist imposed a punctiliar idea on a durative root. An example of this is βλέπω, "I see," which has a basically linear idea; in later Greek it added the sigmatic aorist endings (ἔβλεψα, etc.) to express the punctiliar idea.

---

[3] Compare the English word "snatch," which is punctiliar, and "enjoy," which is linear.

Interpretation of the Tenses

In the interpretation of Greek tenses, there are three pitfalls to avoid. The first is that of equating Greek tenses with English tenses. The tenses of the two languages do not coincide, and the failure to observe this must inevitably lead to confusion in translation. The second is the tendency to read into *Koine* Greek all of the fine shades of meaning present in the tenses of Attic Greek. In the golden age of Attic literature, the Greek language was so facile an instrument of thought and feeling that those who used this language were able to excel all other ancient people in expressing the finer shades of human thought and feeling. But by the time of the writing of the New Testament, the processes of simplification had obscured many of these fine distinctions of the language. There is a third pitfall to avoid. This is the tendency to overlook the significance of the Greek verb roots and the coloring given to the whole idea by the context. Robertson, referring particularly to the importance of verb roots, says, "It has long been clear that the 'tense' has been overworked and made to mean much that it did not mean" (p. 823). Due allowance must be made for the meaning of the verb itself and for the total context.

Three matters, then, must be considered in forming a conclusion as to the translation of particular use of a tense: the significance of the tense, the meaning of the verb, and the contextual relations. And one would do well to bear in mind the words of H.A.A. Kennedy: "In estimating the finer shades of meaning in a mood or tense, different minds will tend to lay different degrees of emphasis on the peculiar force of the construction in its special surroundings . . . [There is] great room for sober, practical judgement in coming to a decision" (*Expository Times,* XII, 1901, p. 344).

LESSON 30

The Present Tense

(Chamberlain, pp. 70-72; Moulton, I, pp. 119-28; III, pp. 60-64; Robertson, pp. 350-53; 864-70.) The present tense is the linear tense; it describes an act as in progress. The idea of time is not prominent except in the indicative, where the present tense denotes progressive or linear action in present time. Outside of the indicative, the present speaks only of kind of action.

Regular Uses of the Present[1]

1. *Descriptive.*—This is the most common use of the present tense for an act in progress. It vividly represents the act as now going on, and is sometimes called the "pictorial present." Example: Κύριε, σῶσον, ἀπολλύμεθα, "Lord, save (us)! We are perishing!" (Matt. 8:25).

2. *Durative.*—Sometimes the present is used to assert that an action or state that was begun in the past is still continuing at the present time. This use is generally associated with an adverb of time, and may best be rendered by the English present perfect. (English, however, has a similar use of the present tense. Example: "Why, he *is* dead and gone these eighteen years.") This use of the present tends to gather up past and present into one word or phrase. It is sometimes called "progressive" present. A good example is in Luke 15:29—'Ιδοὺ Τοσαῦτα ἔτη δουλεύω σοι, "Look, these many years I have been serving you."

3. *Gnomic.*—The present tense may be employed to express a general or timeless truth. Because such statements

---

[1] The categories that follow, both regular and special, are applicable essentially to the indicative mode.

136

are usually axiomatic in character, the temporal element is quite remote.[2] The gnomic present therefore does not affirm that something *is* happening, but that something *does* happen. For example: πᾶς οἶκος *κατασκευάζεται* ὑπό τινος, "Every house is built by someone" (Heb. 3:4).

4. *Iterative.*—The present is sometimes used to describe that which recurs at successive intervals. This is called the iterative present, and may be represented graphically by a broken line (–––––). Examples are as follows: *νηστεύω* δὶς τοῦ σαββάτου, "I fast twice a week" (Luke 18:12). καθ᾽ ἡμέραν *ἀποθνῄσκω*, "I die daily" (1 Cor. 15:31).

Special Uses of the Present

1. *Historical: of an action entirely in the past.*—In historical narrative, the present is sometimes used of past events in order to make them more vivid. This construction is very common in Mark and John. Thus, in Mark 5:15 we find: *ἔρχονται* πρὸς τὸν Ἰησοῦν, καὶ *θεωροῦσιν* τὸν δαιμονι-ζόμενον, "They come to Jesus, and they see the demon-possessed man."[3]

2. *Futuristic: of an action yet future.*—The present tense may sometimes be used of a future event when that event is regarded as certain to come to pass. Thus the "futuristic" present describes with the vividness of a present reality that

[2] The historical, futuristic, and gnomic presents may be either linear or punctiliar in force, depending on the meaning of the verb and the significance of the context. Some grammars recognize as "aoristic present" as a distinct category. See ἀφίενται in Mark 2:5 as an example.

[3] For a different interpretation of the so-called "historical present" see Stephen M. Reynolds, "The Zero Tense in Greek" *(The New Testament Student at Work,* Vol. 2, ed. John H. Skilton). Essentially he argues that "if the context determines that the time of the action was in the past, the present tense could be substituted for the past tense" (p. 100). Thus the historical present functions syntactically as a past tense and is a present only in its superficial form.

which has not yet occurred. (Cf. English, "The ship *sails* tomorrow.") An example of this is found in John 14:3: ἐὰν πορευθῶ . . . , πάλιν *ἔρχομαι* καὶ παραλήμψομαι ὑμᾶς πρὸς ἐμαυτόν, "If I go away . . . , I am coming [= will come] again and will receive you to myself [= take you to be with me]."

3. *Perfective: of perfective action.*—A very limited number of verbs have "perfective" force even in their present tense forms. An example of this is ἥκω, "I have come" (and "am here").

4. *Conative: of an act contemplated or attempted.*—The present tense is sometimes used to describe an action which is not actually realized but only purposed or attempted. Used in this manner, the present suggests that the action tends toward realization. Grammarians call it the "tendential" or "conative" present. Example: διὰ ποῖον αὐτῶν ἔργον ἐμὲ *λιθάζετε*, "For which work of these are you wanting to stone me?" (John 10:32).

Reading Assignment

Translate the following passages, giving special attention to present-tense verbs: Mark 1:40; Luke 7:8; John 15:27; John 20:17; Gal. 1:6, 10.

LESSON 31

The Imperfect Tense

(Chamberlain, pp. 74-75; Funk, pp. 169-71; Moulton, I, pp. 128-29; III, pp. 64-68; Robertson, pp. 882-88; and Zerwick, pp. 91-93.) The imperfect tense, which is used only in the indicative and is a sort of auxiliary to the present tense, denotes linear action in past time. It is much like the continuous past in English, but is by no means identical with it.

It is an especially *descriptive* tense and thus is the proper tense to use in historical narration if one wants to recount events with particular vividness. "The aorist," explains Robertson, "tells the simple story. The imperfect draws the picture. It helps you to see the course of the act. It passes before the eye the flowing stream of history" (p. 883). Or, as the same writer says elsewhere, "The aorist lifts the curtain and the imperfect continues the play" (p. 838).

It may express action in any one of the following ways:

1. *Descriptive.*—This is the use of the imperfect to express continuous action in past time. That is to say, the descriptive imperfect represents an action as going on at some time in the past. It does not indicate whether the process was completed. Example: ἦν γὰρ διδάσκων αὐτοὺς, "For he was teaching them" (Mark 1:22).

2. *Iterative.*—This is the use of the imperfect to express *repeated action* in past time. Example: ἐπορεύοντο . . . κατ᾽ ἔτος, "They used to go . . . every year" (Luke 2:41).[1]

[1] Many grammarians list, in addition to the iterative imperfect, a "customary imperfect." This is a use of the tense to denote an action habitually done. The English "kept on" frequently will bring out the idea, though "used to" may also express it. We have not distinguished the customary as a separate use of the imperfect because it is so similar to the iterative idea.

139

3. *Inceptive.*—This is the use of the imperfect to point up the *beginning of an action,* or to denote an action on the verge of occurring. It implies that the action continues, but the stress is simply on its beginning. To bring out the idea in an English translation, one must ordinarily employ the word "began." Example: ἐδίδασκεν αὐτούς, "He began to teach them" (Matt. 5:2). Some grammarians call this the "inchoative imperfect."

4. *Conative.*—This is the use of the imperfect to express an *action attempted or interrupted.* The inference is that the end of the action was not attained; it only tended toward realization. Example: ὁ δὲ *διεκώλυεν* αὐτὸν λέγων . . . , "But he (John) prevented him saying . . ." (Matt. 3:14). The context brings out that John did actually go on to baptize Jesus, so the meaning must be that he *tried* to prevent Jesus from being baptized. See also Luke 1:59—καὶ *ἐκάλουν* αὐτὸ . . . Ζαχαρίαν, "They were going to call him . . . Zachariah." Some grammarians refer to this as the "tendential imperfect." (Compare the use of the present tense for "an act contemplated or attempted," Lesson 30).

5. *Potential.*—The imperfect is sometimes used to express *a wish politely or hesitantly,* or to express *a wish that is known to be unattainable.* (Compare the indicative for a wish or an impulse, Lesson 20.) This is a special and rather rare use of the tense for an action which is really in present time. Example: *ηὐχόμην* ἀνάθεμα εἶναι . . . ἀπὸ τοῦ Χριστοῦ ὑπὲρ τῶν ἀδελφῶν μου, "I could wish to be accursed . . . from Christ for my brothers" (Rom. 9:3). The wish concerns the present, but the imperfect (in this example) is used to give it an air of unreality. Some grammarians call this the "voluntative imperfect."

6. It is sometimes used with *verbs of obligation, propriety, and necessity.* (Compare the indicative for obligation,

necessity, propriety, Lesson 20.) This is somewhat like the potential imperfect in that it is a *use of the imperfect for present time*. That is to say, the obligation is a present thing. The imperfect possibly is used to suggest that it is an obligation carried over from the past into the present. Compare our use of the word "ought," a past tense of "owe." Example: οὐκ ἔδει καὶ σὲ ἐλεῆσαι τὸν σύνδουλόν σου . . .; "Ought not you also to have mercy on your fellowservant . . . ?" (Matt. 18:33).

Reading Assignment

Translate Mark 1:5, 21; Luke 3:10; 24:32; Acts 7:26; Gal. 4:20.

LESSON 32

The Future Tense

(Funk, pp. 178-79; Moulton, III, pp. 86-87; Robertson, pp. 870-79; Zerwick, pp. 93-96.)

The future is basically a punctiliar tense. Robertson and Davis say "this is due partly to the nature of the case, since all future events are more or less uncertain" (*Short Grammar*, p. 142). It is mainly an indicative tense, not being used at all in the subjunctive, imperative, and optative, and only infrequently in the infinitive and participle.

There are four shades of meaning in the future.

1. *Predictive.*—The most frequent and most natural use of the tense is to express an action expected to occur in the future. Whether it is punctiliar or linear must be determined by a consideration of the meaning of the verb and its context. More often than not, however, this use of the future will be punctiliar in force. Example: αὐτὸς *σώσει* τὸν λαὸν αὐτοῦ ἀπὸ τῶν ἁμαρτιῶν αὐτῶν, "He will save his people from their sins" (Matt. 1:21). The future in this sentence is punctiliar. An example of the linear idea may be found in Phil. 1:18—ἐν τούτῳ χαίρω ἀλλὰ καὶ *χαρήσομαι,* "In this I rejoice; yes, and I will continue to rejoice."

2. *Imperative or volitive.*—The future indicative may be used to express a command. (Compare the indicative of command, Lesson 20.) Example: τέξεται . . . υἱὸν καὶ *καλέσεις* τὸ ὄνομα αὐτοῦ Ἰησοῦν, αὐτὸς γὰρ σώσει τὸν λαὸν αὐτοῦ ἀπὸ τῶν ἁμαρτιῶν αὐτῶν, "She will bear . . . a son, and you are to call his name Jesus, for he will save his people from their sins" (Matt. 1:21). Notice the three future verbs in this example. The first and third express mere futurity; the second is imperative.

3. *Deliberative.*—The future (first person, singular or plural) is occasionally used in questions expressing a deliberative frame of mind. Example: κύριε, πρὸς τίνα *ἀπελευσόμεθα,* "Lord, to whom shall we go?" (John 6:68). τίνι *ὁμοιώσω* τὴν γενεὰν ταύτην; "To what shall I liken this generation?" (Matt. 11:16). (Compare with the deliberative subjunctive, Lesson 21.)

4. *Gnomic or customary.*—The future is sometimes used to express an action which is to be expected under certain circumstances (cf. Funk, p. 178). The element of futurity is very remote in this construction, the reference being to a general or timeless truth, valid for all times. Example: ἕκαστος τὸ ἴδιον φορτίον *βαστάσει,* "Each will [must] bear his own burden" (Gal. 6:5). μόλις ὑπὲρ δικαίου τις *ἀποθανεῖται,* "One will hardly die (i.e. is hardly willing to die) for a righteous man" (Rom. 5:7).

Reading Assignment

Translate the following passages: Luke 1:13; 8:34; 11:5; John 14:26; Rom. 6:14; Eph 5:31; Phil. 3:21; James 2:8.

LESSON 33

The Aorist Tense

(Funk, pp. 171-75; Moulton, I, pp. 129-40; III, pp. 68-74; Robertson, pp. 831-64; Zerwick, pp. 78-80.)

Broadus called Greek an "aorist-loving language," because the aorist is the most prevalent and most important of the Greek tenses. In all the potential modes, and in the expression of past time in the indicative, the aorist was the tense used as a matter of course, unless there was special reason for using some other tense. In the indicative it expresses punctiliar action in past time. Outside of the indicative mode the time element is lost except in a relative sense; the stress is then altogether on the *kind* of action involved.

The Translation of the Aorist Tense

The Greek aorist is not the exact equivalent of any tense in any other language. It may often be translated by the English past tense, but the aorist is much broader than the English past tense. In fact, it is translatable in almost every English tense except the imperfect (continuous past). "The aorist . . . is so rich in meaning that the English labors and groans to express it" (Robertson, p. 848). The context must decide translation.

Aktionsart of the Aorist

The name of the tense is derived from ἀόριστος, "without limit," "unqualified." This suggests that the tense denotes a simple occurrence without defining or describing it; it says nothing about the progress of the action. Moulton observes that it presents "an event as a *single whole,* without regarding
144

the time taken in its accomplishment" (*Introduction to the Study of New Testament Greek*, p. 190).

The Uses of the Aorist Tense[1]

1. *Historical: in historical narration.*—The aorist indicative is the normal tense to use in narrative, and the New Testament writers employ it in such passages unless there is good reason for using some other tense. "Almost any page in the Gospels and Acts will show an abundance of aorist indicatives that illustrate this point" (Robertson, pp. 836, 838). Note, for example, Mark 1:9-11. The historical aorist exhibits the following emphases:[2]

(1) *Ingressive or inceptive.*—The aorist of verbs which denote a state or condition ordinarily emphasizes *entrance* (Moulton, "point of entrance") into that state or condition. This is the ingressive or inceptive emphasis.[3] (Some call it "inchoative.") Compare βασιλεύειν, to reign (be king), with βασιλεῦσαι, to come to the throne (become king); κρατεῖν, to hold, with κρατῆσαι, to take hold of, to seize; ζῆν, to live, with ζῆσαι, to come to life, to enter into life, or to return to life after death. The following are New Testament examples: οἱ ὑμᾶς *ἐπτώχευσεν*, "For your sakes he became poor" (2 Cor. 8:9). ὁ λόγος σὰρξ *ἐγένετο*, "The Word became flesh" (John 1:14). *ἐσίγησεν* . . . τὸ πλῆθος, "The

---

[1] The "uses" of the aorist are largely its uses in the indicative mode.

[2] The three emphases of the aorist tense may be found in any of the modes and in the infinitive and participle, but they are seen most clearly and are perhaps most meaningful to observe in aorist indicatives used in historical narration.

[3] The ingressive aorist should be compared with the inceptive imperfect. The latter implies the continuance of the action; the aorist says nothing about this. The action may in fact continue, but the aorist says nothing about it.

multitude became silent" (Acts 15:12). ἐδάκρυσεν, "He burst into tears" (John 11:35).

(2) *Culminative or effective.*—In some verbs the aorist emphasizes the *end* of the action rather than the beginning. This is ordinarily true of verbs which signify *effort* or *process.*[4] The aorist denotes the success of the effort. This contrasts with the conative imperfect, which suggests that the action was not successfully completed. (Verbs having to do with hindering, shutting, falling, learning, hiding, saving, escaping, etc., lend themselves to the culminative idea.) Examples: ἐγώ γὰρ *ἔμαθον* . . . αὐτάρκης εἶναι, "For I have learned . . . to be content" (Phil. 4:11). καὶ *κλείσας* τὴν θύραν . . . , "And having shut the door . . . " (Matt. 6:6). Some grammars use the words "perfective" or "resultative" instead of culminative or effective.

(3). *Constative.*—Often the aorist simply views an action in its entirety and treats it as a single whole. This is the constative (summary) emphasis.[5] Moulton says it "conceives the action as a whole without reference to the beginning, progress, or end" (I, p. 72). Robertson regards the constative as "merely the normal aorist which is not 'ingressive' nor 'effective' " (p. 832). It accents the middle point. One must remember, however, that the constative aorist may be used of an act which is not a point. In fact, it is often used in connection with verb roots that have a linear idea. In such instances the constative aorist views at a glance the whole

---

[4] The culminative aorist is somewhat similar to the perfect tense, but there is a difference. The culminative aorist indicates the act or process was completed, but says nothing about the continuance of results. The perfect tense combines both of these ideas—a completed act and continuing results.

[5] The aktionsart of the verb root plays a very important role in the ingressive and culminative aorists, but this element is less conspicuous in the constative aorist.

period of time involved, focuses it in a point, and treats it as a point. Examples: ὁ λόγος . . . *ἐσκήνωσεν ἐν ἡμῖν,* "The Word . . . tabernacled among us" (John 1:14). τεσσάρα-κοντα καὶ ἓξ ἔτεσιν <u>οἰκοδομήθη</u> ὁ ναὸς οὗτος, "This temple was built in forty-six years" (John 2:20).

2. *Gnomic: in the expression of a general or timeless truth.*—The "gnomic" aorist describes a fact or truth that is fixed in certainty or axiomatic in character. It represents the action not as something that *did* happen but as something that *does* happen. Perhaps this usage represents the original timelessness of the aorist indicative. Moulton calls it "proleptic." Examples: ἐὰν μή τις μένῃ ἐν ἐμοί, *ἐβλήθη* . . . *καί ἐξηράνθη,* "If any man remains not in me, he is cast forth . . . and is withered" (John 15:6). *ἐξηράνθη* ὁ χόρτος, καὶ τὸ ἄνθος *ἐξέπεσεν,* "The grass withers, and the flower falls off" (1 Pet. 1:24). This use of the aorist is infrequent in the New Testament.

3. *Epistolary: in certain constructions in the writing of letters.*—Sometimes a Greek writer projected himself to the point of view of his readers and used an aorist indicative of an event which, from his own standpoint, was either present or future. In other words, he used the tense that would be appropriate for his readers. At the time of writing the act was present or future, but when the letter was read the act would be past. "This idiom is merely a matter of standpoint. The writer looks at his letter as the recipient will. . . . The most frequent word so used was ἔγραψα, though ἔπεμψα was also common" (Robertson, p. 845). Examples: σπουδαιοτέρως οὖν *ἔπεμψα* αὐτὸν, "Therefore the more quickly I am sending him" (Phil. 2:28). *ἔγραψα* ὑμῖν ὅτι οἴδατε τὴν ἀλήθειαν, "I am writing to you because you know the truth" (1 John 2:21).

4. *Dramatic: as a device for emphasis.*—The aorist

indicative is sometimes employed to describe a present fact or reality "with the certitude of a past event" (Dana and Mantey, p. 198). Adverbs of time are commonly used in such constructions to make clear the present relations of time. The "dramatic" aorist is very similar to the gnomic aorist, but in the latter there is more of the axiomatic. The dramatic aorist is sometimes used of *a state of mind just reached* (ἔγνων τί ποιήσω, "I know what I will do," Luke 16:4); or of *actions which have just happened,* and the effect of which reaches into the present; or it is used of a *result which is on the verge of being accomplished.* Examples: Νῦν *ἐδοξάσθη* ὁ υἱὸς τοῦ ἀνθρώπου, "Now is the Son of man glorified" (John 13:31). κατενόησεν γὰρ ἑαυτὸν καὶ ἀπελήλυθεν καὶ εὐθέως *ἐπελάθετο,* "For he looks at himself and goes away, and immediately forgets" (James 1:24).

Reading Assignment

Translate the following passages, taking particular note of the aorist verbs: Matt. 5:1; 7:28; Rom. 5:14; 14:9; and Col. 4:8.

LESSON 34

The Perfect, Pluperfect, and Future Perfect Tenses

(Dana and Mantey, pp. 200-06; Funk, pp. 175-78; Moulton, I, pp. 140-48; III, pp. 81-85; Robertson, pp. 892-910; Zerwick, pp. 96-99; K. L. McKay, "The Use of the Ancient Greek Perfect Down to the End of the Second Century A.D.," *Bulletin of the Institute of Classical Studies,* 12 (1965), pp. 1-21.)

The Perfect Tense

The perfect tense, which Moulton (*Introduction,* p. 40) calls the most important of the Greek tenses from an exegetical point of view, represents a *completed state* or condition *from the standpoint of present time.* Thus there is a double emphasis in the perfect tense: *present state* resulting from *past action.* In this respect it may be said to combine in itself both the present and the aorist.[1] That is to say, it is both linear and punctiliar. There is no exact parallel to the tense in English.[2]

Four uses (or emphases) of the perfect may be observed:

1. *Intensive.*—The perfect may be used with the force of an

---

[1] Funk observes that "before the form καθέστακα 'I have placed' arose, the same idea was expressed by ἔχω (present) καταστήσας (aorist) . . . " He goes on to explain that "a perfect like πεπληρώκατε may be resolved into ἐπληρώσατε καὶ νῦν πλήρης ἐστίν" (p. 175).

[2] Some grammarians feel there is evidence that the perfect was diminishing in use in the first century A.D. and that the aorist was being used more and more (G. D. Kilpatrick, "The Greek New Testament Text of Today," *The New Testament in Historical and Contemporary Perspective,* ed. H. Anderson and W. Barclay, p. 204). But see Robertson, p. 894, for a different position.

emphatic present. Burton explains that in this construction "the attention is directed wholly to the present resulting state, the past action . . . being left out of thought" (p. 37). Moulton calls these "Perfects with Present Force." Their usage is confined for the most part to a few verbs which use the perfect in this sense only, e.g., πέποιθα, μέμνημαι, ἕστηκα, τέθνηκα. Dana and Mantey, who do not limit the intensive perfect to this narrow range of verbs, explain that "this is the emphatic method . . . of expressing a fact or condition. It is the strong way of saying that a thing *is*" (p. 202).

2. *Consummative.*—The perfect may be used to emphasize the completed action rather than the continuing results. Or, to state it otherwise, the emphasis may be on the completed process by which the results came to be. This type of perfect, found mainly with verbs having linear roots, describes an act or process completed after effort. Examples: *πεπληρώκατε* τὴν Ἰερουσαλὴμ τῆς διδαχῆς ὑμῶν, "You have filled Jerusalem with your teaching" (Acts 5:28). τὸν καλὸν ἀγῶνα *ἠγώνισμαι*, τὸν δρόμον *τετέλεκα*, τὴν πίστιν *τετήρηκα*, "I have fought the good fight, I have finished the course, I have kept the faith" (2 Tim. 4:7).

3. *Iterative.*—The perfect may be used of *repeated action.* This use of the tense, relatively rare in the New Testament, is really only a *special type of consummative perfect.* It, like the consummative perfect, stresses completed action; but something either in the context or in the meaning of the word (or both) indicates that the character of the action was iterative. Robertson calls it the "present perfect of broken continuity" (p. 896). Examples: ὃ ἦν ἀπ᾽ ἀρχῆς, ὃ *ἀκηκόαμεν*, ὃ *ἑωράκαμεν* τοῖς ὀφθαλμοῖς ἡμῶν, ὃ ἐθεασάμεθα καὶ αἱ χεῖρες ἡμῶν ἐψηλάφησαν, περὶ τοῦ

λόγου τῆς ζωῆς, "That which was from the beginning, that which we have heard, that which we have seen with our own eyes, that which we beheld, and our hands handled, concerning the word of life" (1 John 1:1). μή τινα ὧν _ἀπέσταλκα_ πρὸς ὑμᾶς, δι' αὐτοῦ ἐπλεονέκτησα ὑμᾶς, "Did I take advantage of you by any one of the persons whom I have sent unto you?" (2 Cor. 12:17). θεὸν οὐδεὶς _ἑώρακεν_ πώποτε. μονογενὴς θεὸς ὁ ὢν εἰς τὸν κόλπον τοῦ πατρὸς ἐκεῖνος ἐξηγήσατο, "No man has seen God at any time; the only begotten God, who is in the bosom of the father he has declared him" (John 1:18).

4. _Dramatic._—The perfect may be used to _bring a past event vividly into the present._ That is to say, it may be used to describe an event or fact in an unusually vivid and realistic way. Robertson says the dramatic perfect represents an action completed in the past but "conceived in terms of the present time for the sake of vividness" (p. 896). (Compare the historical present and the dramatic aorist.) The dramatic perfect occurs in narrative material and is particularly prominent in John's Gospel. Examples: Ἰωάννης μαρτυρεῖ περὶ αὐτοῦ καὶ _κέκραγεν_ λέγων, οὗτος ἦν ὃν εἶπον, ὁ ὀπίσω μου ἐρχόμενος ἔμπροσθέν μου γέγονεν, ὅτι πρῶτός μου ἦν, "John bears witness of him, and cries out, saying, This was he of whom I said, He that comes after me has become before me: for he existed before me" (John 1:15). κατενόησεν γὰρ ἑαυτὸν καὶ _ἀπελήλυθεν_ καὶ εὐθέως ἐπελάθετο ὁποῖος ἦν, "For he beholds himself, and goes away, and straightway forgets what manner of man he was" (James 1:24). εὑρὼν δὲ ἕνα πολύτιμον μαργαρίτην ἀπελθὼν _πέπρακεν_ πάντα ὅσα εἶχεν καὶ ἠγόρασεν αὐτόν, "And having found one pearl of great price, he went and sold all that he had, and bought it" (Matt. 13:46).

The Pluperfect Tense

The pluperfect tense, found only infrequently in the New Testament, is to the perfect tense what the imperfect is to the present. That is to say, it is an auxiliary to the perfect, differing from it only in the matter of time. The perfect represents a completed state from the standpoint of present time; the pluperfect represents a completed state or condition *from the standpoint of past time.* From this it may be seen that there is in the pluperfect a double emphasis: a past state resulting from previous action. Its uses are the same as the principal uses of the perfect. 1) Of verbs with a decidedly linear emphasis the pluperfect has essentially the force of an imperfect ("intensive" pluperfect). 2) More often it is used to emphasize an action completed and having results continuing up to some point in the past ("consummative" pluperfect). Examples of the former are: John 1:31—καγὼ οὐκ ᾔδειν αὐτόν, "And I knew him not." Acts 1:10—ἄνδρες δύο παρειστήκεισαν αὐτοῖς, "Two men stood by them." John 9:22 contains a good example of the consummative pluperfect: ἤδη λάρ συνετέθειντο οἱ Ἰουδαῖοι, "For the Jews had already agreed."

The Future Perfect Tense

The future perfect represents a *completed state* or condition from the *standpoint of future time.* It sometimes has the force of "a specially emphatic future, denoting the immediate performance of a future action, or the permanence of its results" (Bruce, p. 180).[1] It is rare in the New Testament and is found only in periphrastic form. An example may be found in Matt. 16:19—καὶ ὃ ἐὰν δήσῃς ἐπὶ τῆς γῆς ἔσται

---

[1] F. F. Bruce, *The English Bible.* New York: Oxford University Press, 1970.

δεδεμένον ἐν τοῖς οὐρανοῖς, "And whatever you bind on the earth will have been (or, will be) bound in heaven."

Reading Assignment

Translate John 1:32, 41; Rom. 5:5; and Eph. 2:8. Give careful attention to the tenses used.

UNIT V

Interpreting Participles and Infinitives

LESSON 35

The Participle

(Burton, pp. 53-72; Dana and Mantey, pp. 220-33; Funk, pp. 212-20; Moulton, I, pp. 221-32; III, pp. 150-62; Robertson, pp. 1095-1141; Zerwick, pp. 125-31.)

Nature of the Participle

The very name of the participle indicates that it has a dual character. It is a verbal adjective, sharing in part the characteristics of both the verb and the adjective. As a verb it has voice and tense, may be either transitive or intransitive, and may take adverbial modifiers. As an adjective it is declined in all genders and both numbers, and may be used in any way that an adjective is used. Both verbal and adjectival elements will always be present in the participle, though the emphasis will vary. In one instance the adjectival force will come to the front, and in another the verbal side will be stressed. "But the adjectival notion never quite disappears in the one as the verbal always remains in the other" (Robertson, p. 1101).

Classification of the Participle

The hybrid character of the participle is responsible for much diversity in its treatment by the grammarians.[1] The

---

[1] A summary of the various methods of classifying the uses of the participle may be found in C. B. Williams, *The Participle in the Book of Acts* (Chicago: The University of Chicago Press, 1909), pp. 1-6.

following classification of its uses is based in the main upon that of C. B. Williams (*The Participle,* pp. 1-6).

The Adjectival Participle

The adjectival participle may function attributively, predicatively, or substantively.

1. *Attributive use.*—When the participle is used attributively it functions as *the direct modifier of a noun.* If the article occurs with this construction, it may precede both the participle and the substantive, but it must precede the participle. Only on rare occasions will the article be omitted entirely. An example of the attributive participle with the article may be seen in Col. 1:25—ἐγενόμην ἐγὼ διάκονος κατὰ τὴν οἰκονομίαν τοῦ θεοῦ τὴν *δοθεῖσάν* μοι, "I was made a minister according to the stewardship of God which was given me." An instance of the attributive participle without an article is the following: εἰ ἤδεις . . . σὺ ἂν ᾔτησας αὐτὸν καὶ ἔδωκεν ἄν σοι ὕδωρ *ζῶν,* "If you had known . . . you would have asked him and he would have given you living water" (John 4:10).

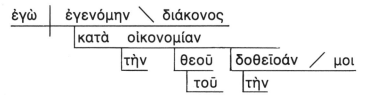

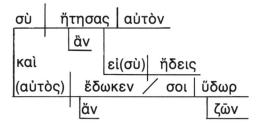

2. *Predicate use.*—This is the use of the participle *after a linking or copulative verb.* In such constructions the participle completes the meaning of the copula and makes a statement about the subject. This is the category for participles in periphrastic constructions and for participles functioning as predicate adjectives. Examples: ἦν *ἐκβάλλων* δαιμόνιον, "He was casting out a demon" (Luke 11:14). ἤμην δὲ *ἀγνοούμενος* τῷ προσώπῳ ταῖς ἐκκλησίαις, I was unknown by face to the churches" (Gal. 1:22).

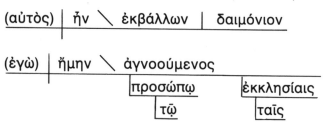

3. *Substantive use.*—The substantive participle is *not accompanied by a noun but itself functions as a noun.* This construction may be anarthrous, but as a rule the article accompanies the participle when it is used in this manner. Examples: ὁ *φοβούμενος* αὐτὸν . . . δεκτὸς αὐτῷ ἐστιν, "The one fearing him . . . is acceptable to him" (Acts 10:35). σὺ εἶ ὁ *ἐρχόμενος*; "Are you the Coming One?" (Luke 7:20).

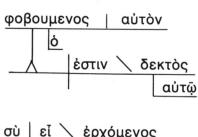

The Circumstantial Participle

The circumstantial participle (sometimes called "adverbial") defines the circumstances under which the action of a verb takes place. Davis says of it: "The circumstantial participle is practically an additional statement added more or less loosely to the verbal notion of the principal verb. It may agree with the subject or object of the principal verb, or with any other substantive or pronoun in the sentence" (p. 105). The circumstantial participle never employs the article. The following ideas² may be conveyed, depending upon the context:

1. The circumstantial participle may be *telic*, expressing the purpose of the action of the main verb. This is the principal use of the future participle. Example: ἐληλύθει *προσκυνήσων* εἰς Ἰερουσαλήμ, "He had come to Jerusalem for the purpose of worshipping" (Acts 8:27). ἀπέστειλεν αὐτὸν *εὐλογοῦντα* ὑμᾶς, "He sent him to bless (lit., blessing) you" (Acts 3:20).

(αὐτὸς) | ἐληλύθει
| εἰς Ἰερουσαλήμ | προσκυνήσων

(αὐτος) | ἀπέστειλεν | αὐτὸν
| εὐλογοῦντα \ ὑμᾶς

2. The circumstantial participle may be *temporal*, in which case it may be translated by "when," "after," or "while."³

---

² The same participle may convey more than one of these ideas.

³ *Antecedent action* relative to the principal verb may be expressed by the aorist or the perfect participle. More often than not, the aorist participle will be used for this. *Contemporaneous action* relative to the main verb is ordinarily expressed by the present participle; but the aorist participle, when used with a main verb in the aorist, often expresses contemporaneous action. *Subsequent action* relative to the main verb may be expressed by the future or the present participle—more often by the future.

(Most circumstantial partciples will have something of the temporal idea in them.) Example: καὶ *ἐλθὼν* ἐκεῖνος ἐλέγξει τὸν κόσμον, "And that one, after he has come, will convict the world" (John 16:8).

3. The circumstantial participle may be *causal,* denoting the ground of the action of the main verb. This is a frequent use of the participle. Example: ἐχάρησαν οὖν οἱ μαθηταὶ *ἰδόντες* τὸν κύριον, "Therefore, the disciples rejoiced because they had seen the Lord" (John 20:20).

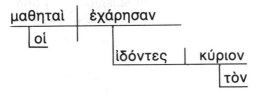

4. The circumstantial participle may be *conditional,* in which case it functions as the protasis of a conditional sentence. Example: καιρῷ γὰρ ἰδίῳ θερίσομεν μὴ *ἐκλυό-μενοι,* "For in due season we will reap if we do not faint" (Gal. 6:9).

5. The circumstantial participle may be *concessive,* expressing the protasis of a concessive sentence. (The

concessive participle refers to an action which is unfavorable to the ocurrence of the action of the main verb. The action of the main verb, then, is accomplished *in spite of* the action of the participle. The English word "though" brings out this idea in translation.) Examples: καὶ *ὀφείλοντες* εἶναι διδάσκαλοι διὰ τὸν χρόνον, πάλιν χρείαν ἔχετε τοῦ διδάσκειν ὑμᾶς τινα, "And although you ought to be teachers because of the time, again you have need that someone teach you" (Heb. 5:12). *λοιδορούμενοι* εὐλογοῦμεν, "Although reviled, we bless" (1 Cor. 4:12).

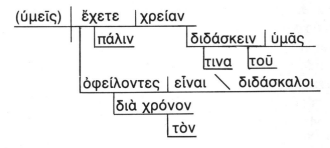

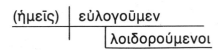

6. The circumstantial participle may be *instrumental,* indicating the means by which the action of the main verb is accomplished. Example: τίς *μεριμνῶν* δύναται προσθεῖναι ἐπὶ τὴν ἡλικίαν αὐτοῦ; "Who by being anxious is able to add to his stature?" (Matt. 6:27).

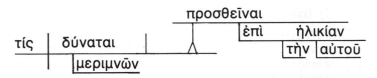

7. The circumstantial participle may be *modal*, denoting the *manner in which* the action of the main verb is effected. Example: παραγίνεται Ἰωάννης ὁ βαπτιστὴς κηρύσσων, "John the Baptist comes preaching" (Matt. 3:1).

Ἰωάννης = βαπτιστὴς	παραγίνεται
ὁ	κηρύσσων

The Supplementary[4] Participle

The supplementary participle forms so close a connection with the principal verb that the meaning of the verb is incomplete without the participle. It is used with verbs of cognition or perceiving (e.g., οἶδα, κατανοέω, γινώσκω, etc.), emotion (χαίρω, ὀργίζομαι, etc.), beginning, continuing, ceasing, and other similar words. It will agree in case, gender, and number with a noun or pronoun in the clause of which it is a part. Example: οὐ παύομαι εὐχαριστῶν ὑπὲρ ὑμῶν, "I do not cease giving thanks for you" (Eph. 1:16). Funk states that the supplementary use of the participle was disappearing in New Testament times.

(ἐγὼ)	παυομαι	εὐχαριστῶν
	οὐ	ὑπὲρ ὑμῶν

The Independent Participle

The independent participle (called participle of "attendant circumstance" by some) is the participle used to form an independent sentence or an independent element within a

---

[4] Some grammars call this use of the participle "complementary." The term "supplementary" rather than "complementary" is here used in order to avoid confusion with the participle used as a predicate complement with a copulative verb. Burton calls this the "substantive participle," explaining that it *names an action*. "It thus performs a function which is more commonly discharged by the infinitive" (p. 175).

sentence. It may be the equivalent of either an indicative or an imperative verb, depending for its precise force on the context in which it is used. Robertson (pp. 1133-34) cautions that no participle is to be explained in this way if it can be properly connected with a finite verb. Examples: <u>ἀποστυγοῦντες</u> τὸ πονηρὸν, <u>κολλώμενοι</u> τῷ ἀγαθῷ, "Abhor the evil, cling to the good" (Rom. 12:9). Μάρκον <u>ἀναλαβὼν</u> ἄγε μετὰ σεαυτοῦ, "Take Mark and bring him with you" (2 Tim. 4:11).

The Participle as Equivalent to a Subordinate Clause

The Greek participle is sometimes the equivalent of a subordinate clause. Generally speaking, all of the above-named uses of the participle may be subordinate clauses with the exception of the predicative participle, the circumstantial participle expressing means and manner, the supplementary participle, and the independent participle. The attributive participle is, as a rule, the equivalent of a relative clause. The substantive participle is generally the equivalent of a substantive clause. The circumstantial participle, with the exceptions noted above, is the equivalent of an adverbial clause. (See Burton, pp. 169, 171.)

LESSON 36

Translation and Syntax

1. Translate 1 Peter 1:1-5.
2. Notes on the text:

Verse 1. πέτρος, a nominative absolute, is the Greek equivalent for the Aramaic Cephas. Jesus gave the name Cephas to Simon when he first met him (John 1:42) and reaffirmed it in the Greek form at the time of the great confession at Caesarea Philippi (Matt. 16:18).

ἐκλεκτοῖς may be taken as a substantive use of the adjective ("elect persons"), or it may be understood as an attributive modifier of the following word ("elect sojourners").

The word Διασπορᾶς appears to be used in a spiritual sense of all the believers addressed in this letter, whether they were Jews or Gentiles. There are numerous references in the letter which suggest that most of the readers were Gentiles, not Jews. Cranfield observes that as "the Church is the new Israel, so also it is a new dispersion."

Verse 2. Three prepositional phrases, κατὰ . . . , ἐν . . . , εἰς . . . , qualify ἐκλεκτοῖς. Some interpreters, however, construe these phrases with ἀπόστολος (vs. 1). Beare relates them to the entire salutation, explaining that they have "a measure of connection with each part of it." Bigg indicates that the entire epistle is a commentary upon πρόγνωσιν θεοῦ, ἁγιασμῷ πνεύματος, and ῥαντισμὸν αἵματος.

Verses 3-5. Some form of the copulative verb (impv., opt., or ind.) is to be supplied after εὐλογητός. Note the prepositional phrases which qualify ἀναγεννήσας (vv. 3-4). Beare thinks εἰς σωτηρίαν (vs. 5) is related both to ἀναγεννήσας and to φρουρουμένους (vs. 5).

3. Indicate the case syntax of:

1) πρόγνωσιν (vs. 2)_____

2) ἁγιασμῷ (vs. 2)_____

3) πνεύματος (vs. 2)_____

4) ὑπακοήν (vs. 2)_____

5) αἵματος (vs. 2)_____

6) ἐλπίδα (vs. 3)_____

7) καιρῷ (vs. 5)_____

4. List and classify all the participles of verses 1-5, using the following table:

Verse	Participle	Related Word		Function
		in form	in sense	
1:3	ἀναγεννήσας	θεός	θεός	adj.—attributive

5. Write out your own translation of 1 Peter 1:1-5.

LESSON 37

Translation and Syntax

1. Translate 1 Peter 1:6-9.
2. Notes on the text:

Verse 6. ᾧ, if construed as masculine, may refer to θεός or χριστός of verse 3 (Hort), or to καιρῷ of verse 5 (Bigg, Robertson, ASV, KJV). If ᾧ is understood as neuter it may refer rather loosely to the entire thought of verses 3-5: "in which circumstances." This is the view of Beare, Selwyn, and others. Viewed in this manner, ἐν ᾧ is practically equivalent to a conjunction, "wherefore." (Compare RSV, "In this;" TCNT, "At the thought of this.")

ἀγαλλιᾶσθε should probably be interpreted as an indicative (ASV, RSV), not as an imperative (Williams, Weymouth). It is a descriptive (pictorial) present denoting continuing joy in the midst of present grief. ὀλίγον is an adverbial accusative of time. δέον is a pres. act. ptc., nom, neut., sing. of the impersonal verb δεῖ, "it is necessary." (Note the uncontracted form. Dissyllabic words frequently are not contracted. This word does, however, contract in some of its forms.) An unexpressed ἐστίν—some manuscripts contain it—should probably be understood with δέον, making it a periphrastic construction. εἰ δέον expresses a first class condition: "if need be," "since it has to be."

Verse 7. The root meaning of δοκίμιον is "means of testing" or simply "testing" (James 1:3). Here it is probably not to be distinguished in meaning from δόκιμον, "genuine," "approved." Beare interprets it to mean "sterling quality," "fine metal." Selwyn translates it "the proven part."

Hort, Selwyn, and Kelly construe πολυτιμότερον κτλ with εὑρεθῇ; Beare takes these words to be a sort of

165

parenthetical explanation of δοκίμιον ... πίστεως. He construes εἰς ἔπαινον κτλ with εὑρεθῇ. δέ gives a concessive sense to the participle δοκιμαζομένου (Robertson).

Verse 8. Note οὐκ with ἰδόντες. The statement concerns a past historical fact, and the negative οὐκ is an attempt to emphasize this (Selwyn). εἰς ὅν is to be taken with πιστεύοντες. This leaves ὁρῶντες without an object, and makes for a slight irregularity.

3. Prepare a grammatical diagram of verses 6-9. (L.R. Elliott's *Syntax in Diagram* is a useful guide. See also the introduction to Unit II of this book.)

4. List and classify all the participles of verses 6-9, using the table on the following page.

5. Write out your translation of 1 Peter 1:6-9.

Verse	Participle	Related Word		Function
		in form	in sense	
1:6	δέον	λυπηθέντες	unexpressed ἔστι	adj.; pred.-periphrastic
1:6	λυπηθέντες	unexpressed subj. of ἀγαλλιᾶσθε	ἀγαλλιᾶσθε	circum.-concession

LESSON 38

Translation and Syntax

1. Translate 1 Peter 1:10-12.

2. Notes on the text.

Verse 10. σωτηρίας, which is incorporated into the relative clause, picks up the σωτηρίαν of verse 9. "Peter lingers upon the word σωτηρία, at each repetition finding something new to say about it" (Bigg). Note the perfective force of the prepositional prefixes in ἐξεζήτησαν and ἐξηραύνησαν.

Verse 11. Bigg explains that "the prophets knew what they prophesied; they knew not, and sought to understand, at what appointed date, or in what stage of the world's history, in what kind of time (ποῖον καιρόν), the prophecy would be fulfilled." Note that ἐδήλου is an imperfect, denoting simple progressive action in past time: "was pointing to." To be more precise, it may be seen as an iterative imperfect: "did from time to time point to." The plural δόξαι probably refers to the successive manifestations of Christ's glory—resurrection, ascension, etc. Note also the attributive position of the several prepositional phrases in verse 11.

Verse 12. διηκόνουν is imperfect indicative. (See note on ἐδήλου in the preceding paragraph.) ἀνηγγέλη is second aorist passive of ἀναγγέλω. The omission of the article before ἄγγελοι makes the construction qualitative—"beings such as angels."

3. What is the subject of ἀπεκαλύφθη (vs. 12)?

4. What is the tense syntax of ἀνηγγέλη (vs. 12)?

5. Make a grammatical diagram of verses 10-12. (Use following page.)

6. List and classify all the participles of verses 10-12, using the format suggested in the preceding lesson.

7. Write out your translation of verses 10-12.

LESSON 39

Translation and Syntax

1. Translate 1 Peter 1:13-16.
2. Notes on the text:

Verse 13. Selwyn observes that διό is the usual particle when an author shifts the emphasis from statement to inference. We should therefore understand this word as introducing a series of exhortations based upon and growing out of the spiritual benefits set forth in 1:3-12. "Girding up" the loins of the mind suggests preparing oneself for strenuous mental activity. νήφοντες primarily denotes abstention from drunkenness, but its reference is wider than this. Beare understands it to include the avoidance of "self-indulgence of every kind." It is here, he says, an injunction "to shun the intoxication of earthly things; true sobriety," he continues, "consists in having the affections 'set on things above, not on things on the earth.' " τελείως likely should be connected with ἐλπίσατε, though Hort, Bigg, Beare, and others take it with νήφοντες. Selwyn, who construes it with ἐλπίσατε, interprets the adverb to mean "unreservedly," "up to the hilt." ἐλπίσατε is ingressive, "fix your hope," "start to hope" (Beare). It "implies the purposeful adoption of a new attitude of mind and heart" (Beare). Aorist imperatives, which carry a note of urgency, are frequent in 1 Peter. ἐπί may express either the ground of the hope (Hort) or the object of it (Bigg). Most interpreters take φερομένην as a passive of φέρω in its usual sense of "bring." Beare thinks it is middle and explains that the middle of this verb may be used "in the sense of swift motion." Accordingly he renders it "coming swiftly."

Verse 14. τέκνα ὑπακοῆς is a Hebraism—ὑπακοῆς being

171

a descriptive (attributive) genitive. (Beare, however, understands ὑπακοῆς to be objective genitive—"children *born for obedience.*") συσχηματιζόμενοι is an independent participle having imperative force, a use of the participle not uncommon in 1 Peter. *Verse 15.* κατά expresses moral conformity to a pattern or standard. Note that τὸν . . . ἅγιον is modified attributively by καλέσαντα. God is holy in the sense that he is separated from all evil. Beare points out that ἀναστροφῇ is "life in relation to others." It is a favorite word with Peter, being used in his two epistles a total of eight times. γενήθητε is ingressive, "begin to be." Hort understands it in the sense of "show yourselves to be."

    3. Indicate the case syntax of:

        1)   ὑποκοῆς (vs. 14)_____

        2)   ἅγιον (vs. 15)_____

    4. Explain the significance of ἔσεσθε (vs. 16).

    5. Prepare a grammatical diagram of verses 13-16. (Use following page.)

    6. List and classify all the participles of verses 13-16, using the format suggested in Lesson 36.

7. Write out your translation of verses 13-16.

LESSON 40

Translation and Syntax

1. Translate 1 Peter 1:17-21.
2. Notes on the text:

Verse 17. ἐπικαλέω in the active and passive means to call out, to call; to name, to give a name to. In the middle (as here) it usually means to call upon (someone for aid), to appeal to, etc. Here the thought seems to be that of *addressing* or invoking God as Father. "πατήρ is one of those words which easily dispense with the article" (Bigg). ἀναστράφητε is second aorist pass. impv. of ἀναστρέφω. The passive perhaps has reflexive force, "conduct yourselves."

Verse 18. ἐλυτρώθητε is first aorist pass. ind. of λυτρόω. The word literally means to deliver or free by the payment of a price, and was used of the redemption of prisoners of war and of the slaves. Its general meaning is to deliver, to rescue. In the New Testament it occurs only three times, but the LXX employs it nearly a hundred times. Beare sees the word in the present context as suggesting a moral transformation, a "deliverance from the vain way of life which their [the readers'] fathers had followed and in which they themselves had been reared." πατροπαραδότου is in the predicate position but is in sense attributive.

Verse 19. Bigg thinks the absence of the article before τιμίῳ αἵματι is significant. It seems to heighten the characterizing force of the construction—"not with corruptible gold but with costly blood." Χριστοῦ is placed last in its phrase for the sake of emphasis.

Verse 20. προεγνωσμένου is perf. pass. ptc. of προγινώσκω. Verbs beginning with a vowel, two consonants, a

175

double consonant (ζ, ξ, ψ), or ρ normally, as here, form reduplication after the analogy of the augment. " 'The foreknowledge of God' conveys the thought of Will and Purpose; that Christ is 'foreknown' means that His work in the world was ordained of God, that the fulfilment of God's purpose for the world was destined to be accomplished through Him . . . ; God 'foreknew' Him in His function as Savior' " (Beare). ἐπ᾽ ἐσχάτου τῶν χρόνων, lit., "in the last of the times," points to the present age as the final epoch of world history.

Verse 21. πιστούς is used in the sense of "believing," a somewhat rare use of the adjective in the New Testament. ἐγείραντα is reminiscent of Peter's numerous references to Jesus' resurrection in his sermons recorded in Acts. ὥστε . . . εἶναι is the equivalent of a result clause.

    3. εἰ (vs. 17) introduces a conditional sentence. Indicate its class.

4. Give the case syntax of:

   1) πατέρα (vs. 17)_____

   2) αἵματι (vs. 19)_____

   3) πίστιν (vs. 21)_____

5. Select all participles in the assignment and give the related word and function of each. (See Lesson 36 for format.)

6. Prepare a grammatical diagram of 1 Pet. 1:17-21. (Use following page.)

7. Write out your translation of 1 Peter 1:17-21.

LESSON 41

Translation and Syntax

1. Translate 1 Peter 1:22-25.
2. Notes on the text:
   Verse 22. ἡγνικότες, a perf. act. part. of ἁγνίζω, denotes a definite act accomplished in the past. But more than this, it emphasizes the existing state or condition growing out of that act. Peter explains that this purification—both act and state—came about through obedience to the truth of the gospel. He further declares that the end and aim of the whole experience was εἰς φιλαδελφίαν ἀνυπόκριτον. Beare, commenting on this terminal accusative construction, observes that "Christians are purified in heart, not for a solitary holiness, but for life in the divine society which is bound together by love."
   Verse 23. Note ἐκ and διά. The former suggests the origin or source of the new birth; διά implies the means by which the new birth is effected. The two participles (ζῶντος and μένοντος) may modify either λόγου or θεοῦ. The context favors the latter construction.
   Verse 24. The quotation from Isa. 40:6-8 points up the contrast between the abiding character of God's word and the transitoriness of earthly things.
   Verse 25. Note the use of ῥῆμα ("utterance") instead of λόγος. εἰς ὑμᾶς, a terminal accusative, is equivalent to a dative of indirect object.
3. Give the syntax of the following:

   1) ἀληθείας (vs. 22)_____

   2) λόγου (vs. 23)_____

3) αἰῶνα (vs. 25)——————————————

4) ὑμᾶς (vs. 25)——————————————

4. Select the participial forms, indicating the usage of each and the word to which each is related.

5. Indicate the tense of each of the following verbs and the significance of each.

1) ἐξηράνθη (vs. 24)————————————

2) ἐξέπεσεν (vs. 24)————————————

6. Prepare a grammatical diagram of 1 Pet. 1:22-25. (Use following page.)

7. Write out your translation of the assigned passage.

LESSON 42

The Infinitive

(Burton, pp. 143-63; Chamberlain, pp. 104-109; Dana-Mantey, pp. 208-20; Funk, pp. 196-212; Robertson, pp. 1050-95; Zerwick, pp. 132-36.)

Nature of the Infinitive

The infinitive, like the participle, is a hybrid. But whereas the participle is a declinable verbal adjective, the infinitive is an indeclinable verbal noun. As a verb the infinitive has voice and tense, may take an object, may be modified by adverbs, and may be used in the expression of verbal ideas. As a noun it may be used in any way a noun can be used. In some examples the verbal aspect will be uppermost, and in some the noun force will be dominant. Both characteristics, however, will always be present. "It is not just a substantive, nor just a verb, but both at the same time" (Robertson, p. 1057).

Uses of the Infinitive

The use of the infinitive in Greek is much wider than the use of the infinitive in English. "It is sometimes translated by the English infinitive, or by the English verbal noun [gerund] in *ing,* and sometimes by the English Indicative, Subjunctive, or even Imperative mood" (Nunn, p. 87). The following categories, based on the arrangement of Nunn (pp. 88-89), suggest the principal uses of the Greek infinitive:

1. It may be used as *a noun element* in the sentence. That is to say, the infinitive sometimes performs the typical noun functions of subject, object, appositive, and modifier. Note the following examples: *Subject:* οὐκ ὑμῶν ἐστὶν <u>γνῶναι</u>

χρονοὺς ἢ καιροὺς, "To know times or seasons is not yours" (Acts 1:7). *Object:* ἤρξατο ὁ Ἰησοῦς <u>ποιεῖν</u> τε καὶ <u>διδάσκειν,</u> "Jesus began to do and to teach" (Acts 1:1). (Some grammars speak of this as "complementary.") *Appositive:* θρησκεία καθαρὰ καὶ ἀμίαντος . . . αὕτη ἐστίν, <u>ἐπισκέπτεσθαι</u> ὀρφανοὺς καὶ χήρας, "Pure and undefiled religion . . . is this, to visit orphans and widows" (James 1:27). *Modifier[1]:* ἔδωκεν αὐτοῖς ἐξουσίαν τέκνα θεοῦ <u>γενέσθαι,</u> "He gave them the right to become [of becoming] children of God (John 1:12). χρείαν ἔχετε τοῦ <u>διδάσκειν</u> τινὰ ὑμᾶς, "You have need that someone teach you" (Heb. 5:12). οὐκ εἰμὶ ἱκανὸς <u>λῦσαι,</u> "I am not worthy to loose" (Mark 1:7).

2. It may be used as *the equivalent of an adverbial clause.* As such the infinitive may express purpose, result, time, or cause. Dana and Mantey (pp. 214-16) describe these as "verbal" uses of the infinitive. They are adverbial notions, however, and it seems better to classify them as such. Note the following examples: *Purpose:*[2] καὶ ἤλθομεν <u>προσκυνῆσαι</u> αὐτῷ, "And we have come to worship him" (Matt. 2:2). *Result:*[3] ἐν παντὶ τόπῳ ἡ πίστις ὑμῶν ἡ πρὸς τὸν θεὸν ἐξελήλυθεν, ὥστε μὴ χρείαν <u>ἔχειν</u> ἡμᾶς λαλεῖν τι, "In every place your faith which is toward God has gone forth, so that we have no need to speak anything" (1 Thess. 1:8).

[1] The infinitive used as a modifier will normally occur with a noun or adjective having to do with authority, need, ability, fitness, etc. In these constructions the infinitive limits the meaning of the noun or adjective, somewhat as a genitive noun may limit such words.
[2] The infinitive expressing purpose may take several forms: the simple infinitive, the infinitive with a preposition (e.g., εἰς, πρός), the infinitive with ὥστε or ὡς, or the infinitive with τοῦ.
[3] The infinitive expressing result may take several forms: the simple infinitive, the infinitive with εἰς, the infinitive with τοῦ (less frequent than the same construction expressing purpose), and the infinitive with ὥστε (the most common construction for the infinitive of result).

Time:[4] μετὰ δὲ τὸ <u>ἐγερθῆναί</u> με, "After I have risen," (Matt. 26:32). *Cause:* οὐκ ἔχετε διὰ τὸ μὴ <u>αἰτεῖσθαι</u> ὑμᾶς, "You do not have because you do not ask" (James 4:2).

3. It may be used as *an independent element,*[5] as in the greetings of letters and in the expression of a command. In these constructions it is equivalent to a principal clause or an independent sentence. An example of the infinitive used in a *greeting:* Ἰάκωβος θεοῦ καὶ κυρίου Ἰησοῦ χριστοῦ δοῦλος ταῖς δώδεκα φυλαῖς ταῖς ἐν τῇ Διασπορᾷ <u>χαίρειν,</u> "James, a servant of God and of the Lord Jesus Christ, to the twelve tribes which are in the Dispersion, greeting" (James 1:1). (Some, e.g. Burton, say the infinitive in a greeting is to be understood as the object of an unexpressed verb, such as λέγω.) An example of the infinitive used to express a *command* may be seen in Rom. 12:15—<u>χαίρειν</u> μετὰ χαιρόντων, <u>κλαίειν</u> μετὰ κλαιόντων, "Rejoice with those who rejoice, weep with those who weep."

Written Assignment: List the infinitives of 1 Thess. 4:7-12, indicating the function of each and the word to which each is related.

---

[4] In relation to the action of the main verb, the infinitive may express *antecedent action* (πρίν or πρίν ἤ followed by the infinitive), *simultaneous action* (ἐν τῷ followed by the infinitive), and *subsequent action* (μετὰ τὸ followed by the infinitive).

[5] Some grammarians speak of this as the "absolute" use of the infinitive.

LESSON 43

Translation and Syntax

1. Translate 1 Peter 2:1-5.

2. Notes on the text. These verses introduce a second doctrinal section (cf. 1:3-12). Up to this point Peter has been thinking mainly of the experience of individual Christians—the blessings and privileges they have in Christ and the responsibilities which grow out of their privileges. In 2:1-10 the point of view is changed somewhat. Here Peter appears to be thinking of the corporate experience of believers. He sees all Christians as making up a society of redeemed people, as composing one great spiritual fellowship. The passage brings out the nature of that fellowship by using three different figures—a family (vss. 1-3), a building (temple) and priesthood (vss. 5-8), and a nation or a people (vss. 9-10).

Verse 1. ἀποθέμενοι is a 2 aor. mid. ptc. of ἀποτίθημι. οὖν connects this section with what has gone before, especially with 1:23 and its reference to the new birth.

Verse 2. βρέφη, a third declension neuter word (pl.), originally meant an unborn child, but it came to be used as a synonym for νήπιος, infant. ἀρτιγέννητα suggests that the readers were recent converts. λόγικος is used in the New Testament only here and in Rom. 12:1. The -ικος ending means "belonging to," "pertaining to." The word λόγικον could mean "pertaining to" the readers' spiritual or rational nature (Hort, Beare; cf., Rom. 12:1). It may also mean "pertaining to the word" (KJV, Bigg, Cranfield). αὐξηθῆτε is 1 aor. pass. subj. of αὐξάνω.

Verse 4. Selwyn points out that λίθος refers to a finished or worked stone (whether a stone used in building or a precious stone), and is to be distinguished from πέτρος, a loose stone, and from πέτρα, a rock. *Verse 5.* οἶκος combines the ideas of house and household, but likely the stress here is on house (temple). The thought is that the people of God are a temple of God. The main emphasis, however, falls on the phrase εἰς ἱεράτευμα ἅγιον. Believers, then, are envisaged "not so much as a temple, but as the *holy priesthood* who inhabit it" (Kelly). ἱεράτευμα, a collective word meaning a company of priests, refers to the vocation of the people of God. This vocation is further defined by ἀνενέγκαι (aor. inf. of ἀναφέρω). Bigg construes οἰκοδομεῖσθε as an imperative (cf. RSV), but probably Hort, Robertson, Selwyn, Beare, Kelly, and others are correct in taking it to be an indicative.

3. Select the participles, indicate the word to which each is related, and classify each according to usage.

4. Explain the usage of ἀνενέγκαι and indicate the word to which it is related.

5. Write your translation of verses 1-5 below:

LESSON 44

Translation and Syntax

1. Translate 1 Peter 2:6-10.
2. Notes on the text:

Verse 6. The motif of Christ as "stone" is continued in verses 6-8, but instead of "living stone" he is thought of as "a chief corner stone." Some think the word ἀκρογωνιαῖος denotes the capstone, the stone placed at the summit of the building as its crown and completion. Others think of it as the great stone put in the angle of the substructure, holding together both the foundation and the walls and giving stability to the entire building.

Verse 7 is Peter's explanation of the promise expressed in verse 6. ἡ τιμή picks up the idea expressed by ἔντιμον (vs. 6). τοῖς πιστεύουσιν carries on the thought of ὁ πιστεύων (vs. 6). The verse "sets in contrast the behavior and destiny of the believing and the unbelieving—to the believing, the honour of a place in the spiritual house; to the unbelieving, shame and disaster, the wreckage of life upon the very Stone which was meant to be its foundation" (Beare). It thus affirms that Christ is "the key to all human destiny and the touchstone of all endeavors; faith in Him leads to honour, unbelief to disaster" (Beare). Selwyn explains ἡ τιμὴ κτλ to mean that "the honour which Christ has by virtue of God's choice is imparted to, and shared by, the faithful" (Selwyn). περιέχει, used as an impersonal verb, means "it stands," "it says."

Verse 8. The antecedent of οἵ[1] is ἀπιστοῦσιν (vs. 7). Its clause explains the reason for the stumbling of unbelievers.

---

[1] Relative pronouns sometimes introduce clauses which have, because of the context, a slight causal significance. This is probably true of this present passage (cf. RSV: "*for* they stumble").

λόγῳ is a dative of direct object and is probably to be construed with ἀπειθοῦντες. εἰς ὃ καὶ ἐτέθησαν should be construed with προσκόπτουσιν, not ἀπειθοῦντες. It is the stumbling (the penalty of disobedience) that is ordained, not the disobedience itself. "The will of God decrees the ruin of unbelief, as surely as the exaltation of faith" (Beare). *Verse 9.* ὅπως introduces a purpose clause. ἀρετάς may mean "excellences," "mighty works," etc. The word was general enough to be used of any preeminence (moral, intellectual, etc.).

3. Select the relative pronouns of this passage and indicate the case syntax of each.

4. Classify the participles of the passage as to related word and function.

5. Write out your translation of 2:6-10 below:

LESSON 45

Translation and Syntax

1. Translate 1 Peter 2:11-17.
2. Notes on the text:
Verse 11 introduces a new ethical section which should be compared with 1:13ff. In the latter passage the duties mentioned are mainly personal and inward. Beginning with 2:11 and continuing through 3:12, they are social and outward. The leading idea throughout this section is submission.

Verses 11-12 are both retrospective and prospective. Verse 11 sums up 1:13—2:10; verse 12 anticipates the emphases of 2:13—3:12.

Verse 11. παροίκους and παρεπιδήμους are not to be sharply distinguished. The former word stresses legal position, a resident alien. The latter word brings out the thought of the transitoriness of one's sojourn. The infinitive ἀπέχεσθαι expresses an indirect command.

Verse 13. ὑποτάγητε (aor. pass. impv. of ὑποτάσσω) introduces the dominant theme of this section (cf. 2:18; 3:1). The phrase διὰ τὸν κύριον is worthy of notice in the interpretation of the passage. Men are to conduct themselves in this fashion "for the Lord's sake."

Verse 14. κακοποιῶν and ἀγαθοποιῶν are both objective genitives.

Verse 15 is parenthetical. ἀγαθοποιοῦντας is in the accusative case to agree with an unexpressed ὑμᾶς.

3. Select the relative pronouns of this passage and indicate the case syntax of each.

193

4. Indicate the mode and tense usage of the following:

1) ὑποτάγητε (vs. 13)_____

2) τιμήσατε (vs. 17)_____

3) ἀγαπᾶτε (vs. 17)_____

5. Write out your translation of verses 11-17.

UNIT VI

Interpreting Clauses and Sentences

LESSON 46

Sentences and Clauses

(Chamberlain, pp. 1-7; Funk-Debrunner, pp. 239-53;
Moulton, III, pp. 291-326; Robertson, pp. 390-445.)

The Sentence
(ὁ λόγος)

"At bottom, grammar is teaching about the sentence"
(Robertson, p. 390). An accurate and thorough understanding of the sentence is therefore essential for the study of any aspect of the Greek New Testament. Our discussion concerns 1) the definition of the sentence, 2) the parts of the sentence, and 3) the classification of the sentence.

Definition

Jespersen defines the sentence as "a (relatively) complete and independent human utterance—the completeness and independence being shown by its standing alone or its capability of standing alone, i.e., of being uttered by itself" (p. 307). Robertson, alluding to the terminology of Giles, calls it the "combination of 'the small coin of language' into an intelligible whole" (p. 390). More simply stated, a sentence is a group of words so related as to express a complete thought. It may be in the form of a statement (*declarative* sentence), a question (*interrogative* sentence), a command (*imperative* sentence), or, occasionally, an exclamation (*exclamatory* sentence).[1]

---

[1] Some grammarians list only three classes of sentences, omitting the exclamatory.

195

Parts of the Sentence

The two essential elements.—Since a sentence must express a complete thought, it must have a subject and a predicate—either expressed or implied. Thus, the *subject,* that part of the sentence concerning which an assertion is made, and the *predicate,* that part of the sentence which makes the assertion about the subject, are the two essential elements in any sentence. Robertson (p. 396) calls them the two radiating foci of the sentence and explains that everything else in the sentence revolves around, and is an expansion of, these elements. The predicate properly contains the substance of the sentence; the subject is subordinate to it and can be expressed in Greek by the mere personal ending of the verb.[2]

Expansion of the subject and predicate.—Both the subject and the predicate may be indefinitely expanded by means of other words, phrases, or clauses. The subject, for example, may be enlarged or extended in numerous ways: 1) by an appositive noun; 2) by the oblique cases of nouns; 3) by adjectives, pronouns, adverbs, or the article; 4) by prepositional phrases; and 5) by subordinate clauses. (See Robertson, pp. 398-400.) In like manner, the predicate is capable of many modifications. It may be qualified 1) by adverbs and adjectives; 2) by prepositional phrases; 3) by subordinate clauses; and 4) if the verb is transitive, by direct and indirect objects (See Robertson, pp. 400-401.)

Elliott (p. 4) compares the sentence to a river: "The thought rises from its source, the subject. It flows through the predicate. It empties into its resting place, the object. On the way it is swayed, colored and directed by its modifiers."

Classification of Sentences

Sentences may be classified in two ways: first, the division

[2] For example, δίδωμι, "(I) give."

into various types may be based on the *mental attitude of the speaker or writer* in expressing his thought. It is on this basis that sentences are spoken of as declarative, interrogative, imperative, or exclamatory. Second, sentences may be classified according to the *number and kind of clauses they contain.* Usually three types are named: simple sentences, compound sentences, and complex sentences.

The simple sentence.—A simple sentence is a sentence containing one main clause and no subordinate clauses. It may be long or short, so long as it has only one subject and one predicate. To be sure, the subject or the predicate or both may be compound, but that does not affect the essential character of the simple sentence.

The compound sentence.—A compound sentence consists of two or more independent clauses, each of which is practically equivalent to a simple sentence. As a rule, the independent clauses in a compound sentence are connected by co-ordinating conjunctions (Robertson, p. 428). Only infrequently is the connective omitted.

The complex sentence.—A complex sentence is one which contains one independent clause and one or more dependent clauses.[3] The independent clause in such sentences is often called the principal or main clause, and each dependent clause is spoken of as a subordinate clause. Other terms used are paratactic (for the principal clause) and hypotactic (for the subordinate clause).

The compound-complex sentence.—Any principal clause of a compound sentence may be modified by a subordinate clause. Hence the definition: a sentence containing two or

[3] This is the conventional definition of the complex sentence, but there is a type of complex sentence in which the principal clause is of itself not clearly apparent; for example, those sentences in which the noun clause is used as subject or object of the principal verb.

more principal clauses and at least one subordinate clause is a compound-complex sentence.

The Clause
(ὁ λόγος)
Definition

Grammarians are not in complete agreement in their use of the word "clause." Bonfante, for example, ("Clause," *Collier's Encyclopedia,* vol. 5, p. 343) defines the clause as a "linguistic unit, whether a sentence or part of a sentence, which without amplification expresses a meaning." As may be seen, this definition is broad enough to include the simple sentence under the designation of clause. Most authorities, however, exclude the simple sentence from this category and restrict the term "clause" to those units of thought which form a part of a complex or compound sentence.

There is disagreement also concerning the place of participles and infinitives in a discussion on clauses. English grammars generally speak of participial and infinitival "phrases" and reserve the term "clause" for those word groups which contain a finite verb. But this is not always true of Greek grammars. Green (p. 172), for instance, lists the use of participles and infinitives as methods of introducing subordinate clauses. Likewise, the entire discussion of subordinate clauses in Chamberlain (pp. 163-93), Dana and Mantey (pp. 268-69), and Robertson (pp. 431-32) assumes that participles and infinitives may be employed in the expression of subordinate clause constructions.

The definition of a clause which is preferred here is as follows: a clause is a group of words normally containing a subject and predicate—though in some instances instead of the subject and predicate, there may be only a verbal—and constituting a member of a complex or compound sentence. It is readily admitted that a group of words containing only a verbal is not, strictly speaking, a clause, but often the Greek infinitive and the Greek participle are at least equivalents of clauses and may be best translated into English as such. Such clause-equivalents may be treated as true clauses.

Types of Clauses

Clauses as related to other elements in the sentence are classified as *independent* and *dependent*.

Independent clauses.—An independent or principal clause is one which could make complete sense if left standing alone. Independent clauses in a compound sentence are spoken of as sustaining a *coordinate* or *paratactic* relation to one another.

Dependent clauses.—A dependent clause, sometimes called a *subordinate* or *hypotactic* clause, is a group of words containing a verb or a verbal and used as a part of another clause—either as a modifier or as a substantive. In other words, *it serves as a single part of speech,* having the function of an adjective, an adverb, or a noun. It may be dependent upon the principal clause, upon another subordinate clause, or upon single words or phrases in either. As a rule, it does not make complete sense when standing alone.

Structural Form of Subordinate Clauses

Attempts to classify subordinate Greek clauses have proceeded along two main lines. Kühner and Gerth (pp. 347-54) and Thumb (pp. 186-200), for example, discuss them from the standpoint of their function in the sentence. Robertson (pp. 953-1049), Chamberlain (pp. 163-213), and Dana and Mantey (pp. 269-303), on the other hand, approach the matter primarily from the standpoint of the form and meaning of the clauses.

Subordinate clauses are united with other parts of the

sentence by relatives, by conjunctions, by participles, and by infinitives. Consequently, these linking words form the basis for the division of subordinate clauses according to their structural form.

Relative Clauses

Relative clauses, the most frequently used of all the subordinate clauses, are introduced by relative pronouns.[4]

Types of relative clauses.—Relative clauses are either definite or indefinite. The definite relative clause describes a particular individual or group and is equivalent to English clauses introduced by "who," "which," or "that." In Greek they are generally introduced by ὅς but occasionally by ὅστις. Indefinite relative clauses describe anyone or anything in general. They correspond to English clauses introduced by "whoever" or "whichever." Though ὅς may sometimes be employed, they are usually introduced by ὅστις. The idea of indefiniteness may be heightened by the use of ἄν in the relative clause.

Relation of the relative clause to the element on which it is dependent.—Each relative clause is basically either adjectival or substantival. That is, it either describes an antecedent by giving an adherent attribute—the more frequent construction—or it performs a typically substantive function within the sentence.

But although a relative clause is always either adjectival or substantival, it may in certain contexts imply a subsidiary adverbial idea, such as cause, purpose, result, condition, or concession. Robertson (pp. 960-62) lists these adverbial

---

[4] Robertson (p. 954), Chamberlain (p. 163), Dana and Mantey (p. 271), Burton (p. 11), and others classify as relative clauses those introduced by relative adverbs as well as those introduced by relative pronouns. But in this manual, relative adverbs will be considered as conjunctions and the clauses they introduce as conjunctive clauses.

notions as special uses of relative clauses and explains that they are not inherent in the relative itself. They are rather due to the logical relation of the relative clause to the rest of the sentence, and hence it is only inferentially that one gets them out of the relative.

Conjunctive Clauses

Conjunctive clauses are those introduced by means of a conjunction.

Kinds of conjunctions.—The superior precision of the Greek language is in part due to the abundance of connectives in its vocabulary. Among these connective words the conjunctions must take the place of greatest importance. They connect words, phrases, clauses, sentences, and even paragraphs, and thus "form the joints of speech" (Robertson, p. 1177). The two kinds of conjunctions—*coordinating* and *subordinating*—make clear the relation between the two elements which they unite. The coordinating conjunctions join paragraphs, sentences, clauses, phrases, or words of equal grammatical value. The most common coordinating conjunctions are καί; τέ and its compounds (εἴτε, οὔτε, and μήτε); γάρ; δέ and its compounds (οὐδέ and μηδέ); ἀλλά; ἤ; μέν; and οὖν.[5] The subordinating conjunctions introduce clauses which are subordinate to some other part of the sentence.[6]

Relation of the conjunctive clause to its principal clause.—The subordinate conjunctive clause may stand in one of three relations to the clause on which it depends: 1) The most frequent use of the conjunctive clause is as an *adverbial modifier,* expressing such ideas as time, purpose, compari-

[5] For a full treatment of coordinating conjunctions, see Robertson, pp. 1178-92.
[6] For a thorough discussion of subordinating conjunctions, see Robertson, pp. 962-1049.

son, result, cause, and condition. 2) In some sentences, the conjunctive clause may be *substantival* and function as subject, object, appositive, or subjective complement.[7] 3) Occasionally the conjunctive clause is *adjectival,* describing some substantive in the sentence.[8]

Participial Clauses

Participial clauses are those which connect with other parts of the sentence by means of a participle. For a discussion of the participle and its uses, see Lesson 35.

Infinitival Clauses

Infinitive clauses are those which connect with other parts of the sentence by means of an infinitive. For a discussion of the infinitive and its uses see Lesson 35.

Grammatical Function of Subordinate Clauses

All subordinate clauses function as grammatical elements within the sentence; that is, they serve as noun-elements, adjective-elements, or adverb-elements. This fact forms the basis for classifying them as substantive clauses, adjective clauses, and adverb clauses.

Substantival Clauses

A substantive clause is a clause used in the sentence as a noun. It may be the subject of the verb, a subjective complement,[9] the object (either direct or indirect) of the verb, or an appositive modifier. Substantive clauses may be relative, conjunctive, participial, or infinitival.

---

[7] These are most often introduced by ἵνα and ὅτι.
[8] For example, local clauses introduced by οὗ and ὅπου.
[9] That is, a predicate nominative.

Adjectival Clauses

Adjectival clauses modify nouns or noun-elements in sentences, as adjectives might do. They are either restrictive or nonrestrictive. The restrictive clause defines the word which it modifies and is essential to the definiteness of its meaning. The nonrestrictive clause describes the word which it modifies but is not essential to its definiteness. In English the nonrestrictive clause is set off by commas.

Adjective clauses are most frequently introduced by the relative pronoun and by the participle, but a conjunctive clause may occasionally be adjectival in force. (See note 8 of this Lesson.)

Adverbial Clauses

An adverb clause qualifies a verbal idea in a sentence. Such clauses usually express cause, comparison, time, purpose, result, condition, or concession. They are commonly introduced by conjunctions, participles, and infinitives.[10] In rare instances, the relative clause conveys a subsidiary adverbial idea (Robertson, p. 960; Dana and Mantey, pp. 272-73). When this is true, the relative clause in reality partakes of the nature both of the adjectival clause and the adverbial clause (Burton, p. 82).

---

[10] For a detailed analysis of the many possible constructions in the expression of these adverbial ideas, consult Robertson, pp. 962-1027; Dana and Mantey, pp. 274-91.

LESSON 47

Translation and Syntax

1. Translate 1 Peter 2:18-25.
2. Notes on the text:
Verse 18. οἱ is the generic use of the article marking out "servants" as a class. ὑποτασσόμενοι is an imperatival participle continuing the idea of ὑποτάγητε of verse 13.
Verse 19. θεοῦ is objective genitive. Note the use of χάρις. A. and G. take it to mean *"that which brings someone (God's) favor."* This is almost the idea of "reward." Beare understands it in its primary sense of " 'excellence'—that which is admirable."
Verse 20. καί likely has consecutive force, "and so."
Verse 21. To suffer without faltering is a part of the Christian's call (εἰς τοῦτο). Christ's sufferings are a pattern, "a writing under" (ὑπογραμμόν) for his followers. (The word was used literally of the model of handwriting to be used by school children. Here it is a model of conduct which is to be copied). The intensity and the character of Christ's sufferings are further illustrated by the series of relative clauses introduced by ὅς (vss. 23-24).
Verse 24. ξύλον means wood, tree, or anything made of wood, such as a cross. ἀπογίνομαι literally means "to get away from," "have no part in," "cease from," but with the dative (as here) means "to die." Kelly renders it "having broken with."

3. Indicate the tense-syntax of each of the following verbs:

1) ἐκλήθητε (vs. 21)_____

2) ἔπαθεν (vs. 21)_____

3) ἀντελοιδόρει (vs. 23)_____

4) ἰάθητε (vs. 24)_____

5) ἐπεστράφητε (vs. 25)_____

4. Using the pattern given in earlier lessons, classify the following participles:

1) ὑποτασσόμενοι (vs. 18)_____

2) ἀγαθοποιοῦντες (vs. 20)_____

5. List the word to which each of the following subordinate clauses is connected.

1) ὅτι (vs. 21)_____

2) ἵνα (vs. 21)_____

3) ὅς (vs. 22)_____

4) ὅς (vs. 23)_____

5) ὅς (vs. 24)_____

6) ἵνα (vs. 24)_____

6. Give the case syntax of the following words:

1) τοῦτο (vs. 21)_____

2) στόματι (vs. 22)_____

3) ξύλον (vs. 24)_____

4) μώλωπι (vs. 24)_____

5) πρόβατα (vs. 25)_____

6) ψυχῶν (vs. 25)_____

7. Write out your translation of verses 18-25.

LESSON 48

Translation and Syntax

1. Translate 1 Peter 3:1-7.

2. Notes on the text:
Verses 1-6 are addressed to Christian wives; verse 7 is addressed to Christian husbands. Observe that in the discussion of the duty of the wife Peter assumes that her husband is a pagan. In the statement about the duty of the husband it is assumed that his wife is a Christian.

Verse 1. ὁμοίως is not to be construed with ὑποτασσόμεναι but with γυναῖκες. That is to say, it is used here simply as a connective and denotes that this paragraph is one of a series (cf. Arndt and Gingrich, p. 571).

Verse 4. ἀφθάρτῳ may be masculine agreeing with an unexpressed κόσμῳ. Or it may be neuter—"that which is incorruptible." πνεύματος may be either possessive genitive or genitive of identity.

Verse 6. The tense of ἐγενήθητε (vs. 6) is difficult to interpret. It may be an instance of the gnomic (timeless) aorist. If so, it should be translated by the English present, "you show yourselves to be." If it is historical aorist, the force of it is to point back to the time of conversion.

Verse 7. ὁμοίως is a connective, just as it is in verse 1. ζωῆς is likely a genitive of identity. εἰς τό with the infinitive expresses purpose.

3. Select the participles, indicating the usage of each and the word to which each is related.

4. Write out your translation of verses 1-7.

LESSON 49

Translation and Syntax

1. Translate 1 Peter 3:8-17.
2. Notes on the text:
Verse 8. τὸ δὲ τέλος introduces the conclusion of the section begun at 2:13. It is an adverbial accusative and may be literally translated "now with reference to the end." The sense, however, is like our "to sum up," or "finally." The πάντες is inclusive of all the different groups mentioned in the preceding verses—servants, wives, and husbands.
Verse 9. Note the employment of ἀντί. It is the preposition which is used in Mark 10:45 concerning Jesus' giving himself "a ransom instead of the many." τοὐναντίον, an adverb meaning "on the other hand," is an instance of *crasis* (mixing or combination). The word represents τὸ ἐναντίον. Crasis, which is rare in the New Testament, affects καί or the article and a second word. Other examples are κἀγώ (for καὶ ἐγώ) and τοὔνομα (for τὸ ὄνομα). Note that it sometimes involves omission of vowels (as in κἀγώ) and sometimes involves contraction (as in τοὐναντίον and τοὔνομα). Observe also that the breathing mark of the second word is retained. This mark is called the *coronis*.
Verse 10. τοῦ with the inf. probably expresses purpose. It may be seen, however, as an ablative construction following a verb of hindering (παυσάτω). If the latter interpretation is followed, the negative μή must be understood as redundant.
Verse 13 speaks of the pursuit and practice of goodness, but suffering, specifically suffering for righteousness, is the dominant idea of the section introduced at verse 13. ἀγαθοῦ is an objective genitive.
Verse 14 is an example of an elliptical fourth class

conditional sentence. The protasis is expressed; the apodosis is unexpressed. (Compare with verse 17.) ταραχθῆτε is from ταράσσω.
3. Select the verbals of vs. 10-12 and indicate the related word and usage of each.

4. Give the modes of the following and the usage of each:

1) κληρονομήσητε (vs. 9)_____

2) παυσάτω (vs. 10)_____

3) πάσχοιτε (vs. 14)_____

4) φοβηθῆτε (vs. 14)_____

5) καταλαλεῖσθε (vs. 16)_____

6) θέλοι (vs. 17)_____

5. Explain the case syntax of the following:

1) χείλη (vs. 10)_____

2) ἀγαθοῦ (vs. 13)_____

3) φόβον (vs. 14)_____

4) κύριον (vs. 15)_____

5) λόγον (vs. 15)_____

6. Pick out all of the conditional sentences and indicate the class to which each belongs.

7. Write out your translation of verses 8-17.

LESSON 50

Translation and Syntax

1. Translate 1 Peter 3:18-22.
2. Notes on the text:
This passage gives encouragement (note ὅτι, vs. 18) for carrying out Peter's previous admonition. When believers are called upon to suffer for righteousness, let them remember that Christ also suffered. Indeed, he died, the righteous for (ὑπέρ, vs. 18) the unrighteous. ἅπαξ (vs. 18) does not mean "once upon a time" but rather "once for all." Christ's death does not need to be, in fact cannot be, repeated.

The thought, not the translation, of this passage is difficult. See Robertson's *Word Pictures* for a concise but helpful statement of the problem and its interpretation. Selwyn, Bigg, and Beare give detailed discussions of the Greek text. Kelly's interpretation, though based on the English text, offers penetrating insights. The following questions must be considered: Who are the spirits in prison? When, how, and for what purpose did Christ preach to them?

3. The subordinate clauses of this passage are important to its interpretation. Select them and indicate the usage of each.

4. The participles of this passage are significant to its interpretation. Select them, indicate their tenses, and show the related word and usage of each.

5. Indicate the word to which each of the following is related:

1) ᾧ (vs. 19)_____

2) ὅ (vs. 21)_____

3) ὅς (vs. 22)_____

6. Write out your translation of verses 18-22.

LESSON 51

Translation and Syntax

1. Translate 1 Peter 4:1-11.

2. Notes on the text:

Verses 1-6 show that the sufferings of Christ are to be more than an example to the believer; they are to be a moral and practical power in his life.

Verse 1. οὖν, which begins the passage, refers back to 3:18. It "draws and applies the main lesson of 3:18-22, the fact that Christ suffered for us" (Robertson). A. and G. take ἔννοιαν to mean "insight." σαρκί (second occurrence) is generally understood as a locative of sphere, though there are some who take it to be a dative of reference (cf. 2:24). ὅτι ὁ παθὼν ... ἁμαρτίας is parenthetical.

Verse 2. Construe εἰς τὸ ... βιῶσαι with ὁπλίσασθε (vs. 1).

Verse 3. The three perfects of verse 3 emphasize the thought that the readers' past "is a closed chapter" (Beare). Robertson takes πεπορευμένους to be a substantive use of the participle, functioning here as an accusative of reference with the infinitive κατειργάσθαι.

Verses 5 and 6 raise two principal questions: 1) Who are the dead? 2) When was the gospel preached to them?

Verse 7 indicates that the judgment of which Peter speaks is an imminent matter (cf. 1:20).

Verse 8. Peter's reference to love covering a multitude of sins likely means that love is willing to forgive again and again.

Verses 9-11. The concluding verses of this paragraph suggest that the life regulated by grace cannot reflect grumbling, only goodness.

3. Give the case, related word, and function of the following participles:

1) παθόντος (vs. 1)_____

2) παρεληλυθώς (vs. 3)_____

3) συντρεχόντων (vs. 4)_____

4) βλασφημοῦντες (vs. 4)_____

4. Indicate the related word and function of each of the following:

1) βιῶσαι (vs. 2)_____

2) κατειργάσθαι (vs. 3)_____

3) κρῖναι (vs. 5)_____

5. Classify these clauses according to form and function:

1) ὅτι (vs. 1)_____

2) εἰς τό (vs. 2)_____

3) ἵνα (vs. 6)_____

4) ὅτι (vs. 8)_____

5) εἴ (vs. 11)_____

6. Write out your translation of verses 1-11.

LESSON 52

Translation and Syntax

1. Translate 1 Peter 4:12-19.

2. Notes on the text:

This section continues Peter's emphasis upon suffering as a valid experience of the Christian life. (Cf. Rom. 8:17 where Paul speaks of "suffering with Christ.")

Verse 12. ξένου . . . συμβαίνοντος is a genitive absolute. ὡς indicates that what is stated in the participle is the alleged (false) reason for the action of the main verb (ξενίζεσθε). What is happening to them is not a strange thing.

Verse 13. καθό is an adverb (conjunction) of degree, "in so far as," "to the degree that."

Verse 14. Observe the repetition of the article τό—"the (Spirit) of glory and the Spirit of God" (lit., "the of-glory and the of-God Spirit").

Verse 17. A verb (probably ἐστίν) is to be supplied before ὁ καιρός. The article τοῦ goes with the infinitive ἄρξασθαι. The whole infinitive construction is in loose apposition with καιρός—a sort of genitive of identity. κρίμα is accusative of reference.

Verses 18 and 19 emphasize the imminent sufferings of Christians and show that the only reasonable action is for them to commit—the word is a banking term—their souls to God. καί (vs. 19) should be taken with ὥστε—"wherefore also." The two words suggest that this verse is a summing up of the whole preceding paragraph.

3. Indicate the usages of the following modes:

1) ξενίζεσθε (vs. 12)_____

2) χαίρετε (vs. 13)_____

3) ὀνειδίζεσθε (vs. 14)_____

4) πασχέτω (vs. 15)_____

5) αἰσχυνέσθω (vs. 16)_____

4. What is the syntax of the following clauses?

1) ἵνα (vs. 13)_____

2) εἰ (vs. 14)_____

3) ὅτι (vs. 14)_____

4) εἰ (vs. 16)_____

5) ὅτι (vs. 17)_____

6) εἰ (vs. 18)_____

5. Give the case syntax of these words:

1) ὑμῖν (vs. 12)_____

2) πνεῦμα (vs. 14)_____

3) ὑμῶν (vs. 15)_____

4) καιρός (vs. 17)_____

5) κρίμα (vs. 17)_____

6. Write out your translation of verses 12-19.

LESSON 53

Translation and Syntax

1. Translate 1 Peter 5:1-5.
2. Notes on the text:
Verse 1. οὖν shows there is a close connection with the final verses of chapter 4. "The fiery trial with its temptations to apostasy, the judgment beginning at the house of God, the challenge to Christians to commit their souls in well-doing to a faithful Creator, as they are called to suffer—these things make all the more urgent the need for faithfulness in pastoral care" (Cranfield).

Πρεσβυτέρους emphasizes the dignity of the pastoral office. Μάρτυς and ποιμάνατε (vs. 2) suggest the nature of the pastor's work. The primary meaning of μάρτυς is not "eye-witness" but "one who testifies." It is generally translated "witness," but the KJV renders it "martyr" in Acts 22:20; Rev. 2:13; 17:6. The martyr was one who "bore the supreme and unanswerable testimony" (Beare).

Verse 2. τὸ ἐν ὑμῖν ποίμνιον speaks of that part of God's flock committed to a particular elder's care. The construction emphasizes that the whole flock belongs to God.

Verses 2b and 3 delineate the minister's manner of service, negatively and positively.

Verse 4 indicates a personal relationship to the Chief Shepherd and an expectation of reward from him. Beare calls attention to the fact that the "crown" was given to two classes of persons in Greek cities: 1) to athletes who were victorious in the games; 2) to citizens who distinguished themselves in public service.

Verse 5. Ὁμοίως denotes a transition to a new topic of discussion (cf. 3:1). Πρεσβυτέροις is here used with reference to aged persons and not with reference to the office of elder. κομιεῖσθε is Ionic future of κομίζομαι.

3. Give the syntax of the following:

1) παθημάτων (vs. 1)_____

2) ἀποκαλύπτεσθαι (vs. 1)_____

3) ποιμνίου (vs. 3)_____

4) στέφανον (vs. 4)_____

5) ταπεινοῖς (vs. 5)_____

4. The following are participial forms. Indicate the usage of each.

1) μελλούσης (vs. 1)_____

2) κατακυριεύοντες (vs. 3)_____

3) φανερωθέντος (vs. 4)_____

5. Write out your translation of verses 1-5.

LESSON 54

Translation and Syntax

1. Translate 1 Peter 5:6-14.

2. Notes on the text:

Verses 6-11 continue Peter's discussion of the Christian's responsibility in the midst of trials. In verses 1-4 he set forth the duty of elders. In verse 5a he mentioned the duty of younger believers. In 5b-11 the discussion concerns all believers. They are exhorted to humility, sobriety, watchfulness, and resistance to the devil.

Verse 6. ταπεινώθητε may be interpreted "allow yourselves to be humbled," that is, "accept your humiliation" (Selwyn). Peter appears to have in mind the sufferings discussed in 4:12-19. The reference to the "mighty hand of God" is to give the readers "assurance that God has not forsaken them in their tribulation or left them unprotected in the hands of their enemies. His 'mighty hand' is over them—for judgment, but also for their protection" (Beare).

καιρῷ is almost equivalent to our "in good time." Beare understands it in the sense of "appointed time."

Verse 7. μέλει is an impersonal verb and may literally be translated "it is a care." God is concerned about our troubles.

Verse 9. στέρεοι speaks of "a flint-like resolution" (Selwyn). εἰδότες with an infinitive normally would mean "knowing how to," but Selwyn feels it is better to take it here in the simple sense, "knowing." (See Beare for a presentation of the view that the construction means "knowing how to.") τὰ αὐτὰ τῶν παθημάτων is an unusual construction. Selwyn takes it to mean "the same tax of sufferings." παθημάτων is probably a genitive of identity.

Verse 10. καταρτίζω was sometimes used of mending nets

222

and of repairing and refitting a damaged ship. Peter declares, by his use of this word, that God will repair the damage done to his readers by the ravages of persecution. Verses 12-14 conclude Peter's letter. Note the part played by Silvanus in the writing of this letter (vs. 12). *Verse 12.* Δι' ὀλίγων is an idiom for "briefly." The literal meaning is "through few (words)." ἔγραψα is epistolary aorist.

Verse 13 presents two interpretative problems which revolve around the expression "elect lady" and the term "Babylon." Some commentators insist that the "elect lady" is Peter's wife while others are equally sure that the expression refers to the church in "Babylon." The latter term may be a reference to the actual Babylon (in Mesopotamia) or the mystical Babylon (Rome) as described in John's Revelation. (There was a Babylon in Egypt, but it was little more than a Roman military outpost.) Bigg, Robertson, Selwyn, and Beare believe Babylon to be a reference to Rome.

3. How are the following imperatives used?

1) ταπεινώθητε (vs. 6)_____

2) Νήψατε (vs. 8)_____

3) γρηγορήσατε (vs. 8)_____

4) ἀντίστητε (vs. 9)_____

5) ἀσπάσασθε (vs. 14)_____

4. Give the syntax of these infinitives:

1) καταπιεῖν (vs. 8)_____

2) ἐπιτελεῖσθαι (vs. 9)_____

3) εἶναι (vs. 12)_____

5. Indicate the interpretative significance of the following clauses:

1) ἵνα (vs. 6)_____

2) ὅτι (vs. 7)_____

3) ὡς (vs. 8)_____

6. Write out your translation of verses 6-14:

APPENDIX I

Helps for Identifying Verbs

The Finite Verb

1. Learn the *principal parts* of as many verbs as possible; there is no substitute for this. The principal parts of a verb are the first person singular indicative forms of every system used by that verb. Example: λύω, λύσω, ἔλυσα, λέλυκα, λέλυμαι, ἐλύθην.

2. Study the *stem,* and remember that there are *tense* stems and *verb* stems. Sometimes the tense stem and the verb stem are the same. For example, the verb stem of λύω is λυ- and the present tense stem is also λυ-. But often tense stems, by means of prefixes and other modifications, are different from verb stems. In λείπω, for instance, the verb stem is λιπ-, the present tense stem is λειπ-, the aorist tense stem is λιπ-, and the perfect tense stem is λελοιπ-.

3. Look for *other distinguishing marks,* such as:

1) *Augment.* If the verb has an augment it is either an *aorist, imperfect,* or *pluperfect* indicative. These are the secondary (historical) tenses and carry the augment in the indicative. The augment is either *syllabic* (as in ἔλυον) or *temporal* (as in ἠγάπησα). If an indicative verb has no augment, it is a *present, future, perfect,* or *future perfect.* These are the primary tenses. The primary tenses have primary endings in the indicative; the secondary tenses have secondary endings in the indicative. (Note: the terms "primary" and "secondary" apply only to the tenses of the indicative mode.)

2) *Tense suffix.* These are as follows:
Present: None
Imperfect: None. (The imperfect is made on the present stem and is a part of the present tense system.)

Future: -σ- (as in λύσω). Remember that the liquid futures)o not have the -σ-. These insert an ε, which contracts with the ending and alters the accent. For example, the future of κρίνω is κρινέω-κρινῶ. Compare also βαλῶ, ἀγγελῶ, μενῶ, etc. There are a few primitive futures like φάγομαι (present, ἐσθίω).

First aorist active and middle: -σα- (as in ἔλυσα). Remember that the liquid aorists expel the -σ- (as in ἤγειρα and ἔμεινα). Liquid aorists regularly lengthen the stem vowel. Thus μένω becomes ἔμεινα.

Second aorist active and middle: None (Example: ἔλιπον and ἐλιπόμην). But -κα is the suffix in the "Kappa" aorist, which is to be classified as a second aorist. Example: ἔδωκα, aorist of δίδωμι). The strong or root aorists, like ἔστην and ἔγνων are second aorists. Note the presence of -α- in some second aorists, as εἶπαν, and εἴδαμεν.

First perfect active: -κα- (as in λέλυκα).

Second perfect active: -α- (as in γέγονα).

Perfect middle and passive: Has no tense suffix. The endings are added directly to the reduplicated verb stem, as λέλυμαι and γέγραμμαι.

First pluperfect active: -κει- as in (ἐ)λελύκειμεν.

Second pluperfect active: -ει- as in (ἐ)γεγόνειμεν.

Pluperfect middle and passive: Has no tense suffix. The endings are added directly to the reduplicated stem, as in (ἐ)λελύμην.

Future perfect: -σ- added to a reduplicated stem, as in λελύσομαι and γεγράψομαι.

3) *Voice suffix.*

First aorist passive: -θη- in the indicative (as in ἐλύθην), the imperative (as in λύθητι), and the infinitive (as in λυθῆναι). -θε- is used in the subjunctive (as in λυθῶ), the optative (as in λυθείην), and the participle (as in λυθείς).

Second aorist passive uses -η- wherever the first aorist used -θη- and -ε- wherever the first aorist uses -θε-.
First future passive: -θησ- as in λυθήσομαι.
Second future passive: -ησ- as in γραφήσομαι.
4) *Reduplication.* Usually the reduplication of the verb stem indicates a perfect, but there are a few reduplicated presents, like δίδωμι and reduplicated aorists, like ἤγαγον. In the perfect, reduplication runs through all the modes, the infinitive, and the participle—and in this is *unlike* augment. The perfect indicative of λύω is λέλυκα; the subjunctive is λελύκω or λελυκώς ὦ, the infinitive is λελυκέναι; the participle is λελυκώς. Note that the reduplication in some verbs is like augments, as ἔγνωκα (γινώσκω), ἔσπαρμαι (σπείρω), ἔστηκα (ἵστημι), etc.
5) *Mode Sign.* Remember that the subjunctive, the imperative, and the optative never have the augment.
The *indicative* has no distinctive mode sign. In thematic forms the vowel is short in the indicative, as in λύομεν.
The *subjunctive* uses the lengthened form of the thematic vowel, ω/η, as its mode sign, as in λύωμεν.
The *imperative* has no distinctive mode sign. The thematic forms use the short vowel ε/ο. To recognize the imperative you must know its personal endings.
The *optative* uses -ιη- in nonthematic forms, as in λυθείην, and -ι- in thematic forms, as in λύοιμι and λύσαιμι [the -α- here serves as a thematic vowel.]
4. Give attention to the personal endings. They indicate:
1) The person of the verb.
2) The number of the verb.
3) The voice of the verb.
The *active voice* uses the active endings.
The *middle voice* uses the middle endings, as in λύομαι.
The *passive voice* uses the middle endings, in the present,

as in λύομαι; the imperfect, as in ἐλυόμην; the perfect, as in λέλυμαι; and the future passive, as in λυθήσομαι.

The aorist middle may always be distinguished at once from the aorist passive, since the aorist middle uses middle endings, as in ἐλυσάμην, and the aorist passive uses active endings, as in ἐλύθην.

4) In the indicative they tell whether the tense is primary or secondary.

The Infinitive

1. The infinitive has *no augment;* but it does have reduplication in the perfect.
2. Observe the tense stem.
3. Determine the voice by the ending. In the infinitive these are as follows: -ναι in the present and second perfect active of -μι verbs, as τιθέναι and ἑστάναι; and in first and second aorist passive, as λυθῆναι and γραφῆαι.

-εναι in the perfect active, as in λελυκέναι.

-αι in the first aorist active, as in λῦσαι.

-σθαι in the present, future, and perfect middle and passive, as λύεσθαι, λύσεσθαι, λελύσθαι, and λυθήσεσθαι.

-εν in the present and second aorist active of -ω verbs and all active futures, as λύειν, λυπεῖν and λύσειν. The -εν of the ending contracts with the thematic vowel (ε) to make -ειν.

The Participle

1. The participle has *no augment,* but it does have reduplication in the perfect.
2. The formative element of all active participles (except the perfect), and of the passive participles of the first and second aorist, is -ντ. This is seen in, λύων (for λύοντι),

λυθείς (for λύθεντς), and τιθείς (for τίθεντς), and in λύοντος and τιθέντος.

3. The perfect active participle is a specialized formation. The first perfect participle of λύω is λελυκώς. The second perfect participle of γίνομαι is γεγονώς.

4. The formative element in all middle and passive participles (except the aorist passive) is -μεν-. It is seen in the following forms: λυόμενος, λυσάμενος, and λελυμένος.

5. The gender and number of the participle will be determined by its case endings.

General Suggestions

1. Be on the alert for the contract verbs. The more common ones are ἀγαπάω, τιμάω, ποιέω, πληρόω, φιλέω, etc.

Contraction takes place only in the present and imperfect tenses, and it is only in these tenses that the contract verbs are different from other verbs.

2. Master the *personal endings*. The personal ending of verb helps designate the voice, person, number, and (in the indicative) the tense.

3. In parsing the verbs, use this order: tense, voice, mode, person, number. Thus λύει is the present, active, indicative, third person, singular of λύω.

4. Develop the habit of analyzing the verb forms which you locate.

Illustrations:

ἐλύομεν may be divided into parts: ἐ-λύ-ο-μεν; ἐ- is the augment; -λυ is the tense stem (the verb stem as well); -ο- is the connecting vowel; -μεν is the secondary active first person plural personal ending. The *augment* tells that this form must be either the imperfect, the aorist, or the pluperfect; also that it must be the indicative mode, for the subjunctive, the imperative, and the optative are unaugmented. The *tense stem* -λυ- is the same as the present stem, indicating that this is an imperfect, the imperfect being built on the present stem. The *connecting vowel* -ο- is the short vowel, indicating that this form is an indicative. (It cannot be subjunctive, infinitive, imperative, or participle, because it has an augment.) The *personal ending* -μεν shows that this is a first person plural, and that the voice is active (keeping in mind that the aorist passive also uses active endings). The primary ending is the same as the secondary here, so the ending does not tell whether the tense is primary or secondary, but the augment tells this. We conclude, therefore, that this form is the imperfect, active, indicative, first person, plural of λύω.

λελυμένος may be divided into parts: λε-λυ-μεν-ος; λε- is the *reduplication;* -λυ- is the verb stem; λελυ- is the tense stem; -μεν- is the participial suffix; -ος is the case ending. The *reduplication* λε- shows that is a perfect. The formative suffix -μεν- shows that it is a middle or passive participle. The case ending -ος shows that it is the nominative, masculine singular. We conclude, therefore, that this is the perfect, middle or passive participle, masculine, nominative, singular of λύω.

5. Develop the habit of writing down and looking up every verb form that you cannot locate. Learn the present indicative active first person singular (or the middle, if the verb is defective) of every verb, and then take the trouble to observe the peculiarities of individual verbs. Again, learn the principal parts of as many verbs as possible.

APPENDIX II

Guidelines for Translation

To translate is to turn the words of one language into the words of another language. To translate Greek into English is to turn a Greek sentence into an English sentence meaning exactly—so far as it is possible—what the Greek sentence means. The English sentence may or may not be a word-for-word translation of the Greek. In fact, the most widely used modern translations are sense for sense, not word for word. The beginning student, however, should make a word-for-word translation wherever this is possible.

The following steps are suggested as a good procedure to follow in translating Greek into English:

1. Be sure that you have a working knowledge of English grammar. It is entirely presumptuous for one who does not understand his own language to attempt to translate a language which is not native to him. If you feel the need for a review of English grammar, see Homer C. House and Susan E. Harman, *Descriptive English Grammar* (Prentice-Hall, Inc.); George D. Curme, *English Grammar* (Barnes and Noble); James C. Fernald, *English Grammar Simplified* (Funk & Wagnalls Co.); Walsh, *Plain English Handbook* (McCormack-Mathers Publishing Co.); or Frank X. Braun, *English Grammar for Language Students* (Edwards Brothers, Inc., Ann Arbor, Mich.).

2. Take up each word in order and as nearly as possible translate it in the order in which it appears in the Greek sentence. In an inflected language like the Greek it is not necessary to indicate the grammatical dependence of words by their order in the sentence. Accordingly there are no unalterable rules that may be insisted on in the order of words

in a Greek sentence. The prevailing usage, however, indicates that the subject and its adjuncts normally come first, then the predicate and its modifiers follow.

3. Endeavor to understand thoroughly each word before you leave it—its form, its meaning, its use in the particular passage under consideration. To do this, you must know the fundamentals of the Greek language, such as declension, conjugation, etc. In addition to this you must make frequent use of a good grammar and a good lexicon. The grammar will help you to understand syntax—the relationship of words, phrases, and clauses to one another. The lexicon will enable you to get at the exact meanings of words.

4. When you have studied thoroughly each word in a sentence and feel that you have a grasp of the meaning of the passage, you are ready to translate the total idea into English. Do not attempt to translate any Greek passage into English until you know what the passage means.

5. Do not use commentaries or other translations except to check the conclusions which you have reached independently in your own study.

6. Keep a notebook containing your own translation and the pertinent information about words which are not familiar.

7. Go over the passage a second or third time, consulting your notes when necessary and comparing your translation with that given in a version such as ASV or NASB.

Bibliography

Grammars, Lexicons, and Related Works

ARNDT, W. W., and GINGRICH, F. W. *A Greek-English Lexicon of the New Testament and Other Early Christian Literature.* A translation and adaptation of W. Bauer's *Griechisch-Deutsches Wörterbuch.* Chicago: University of Chicago Press, 1957.

BAKKER, W.F. *The Greek Imperative.* Amsterdam: Adolf M. Hakkert, 1966.

BLASS, F. and DEBRUNNER, A. *A Greek Grammar of the New Testament and Other Early Christian Literature.* Trans. and rev. by Robert W. FUNK. Chicago: University of Chicago Press, 1961.

BROWN, COLIN (ed). *The New International Dictionary of New Testament Theology.* Grand Rapids: Zondervan, 1975.

BURTON, ERNEST DEWITT. *Syntax of the Moods and Tenses in New Testament Greek.* Third Edition. Edinburgh: T. & T. Clark, n.d.

CHAMBERLAIN, WILLIAM DOUGLAS. *An Exegetical Grammar of the Greek New Testament.* New York: Macmillan Co., 1948.

COLWELL, ERNEST CADMAN and TUNE, ERNEST W. *A Beginner's Reader-Grammar for New Testament Greek.* New York: Harper & Row, Publishers, n.d.

DANA, H.E. and MANTEY, J.R. *A Manual Grammar of the Greek New Testament.* New York: Macmillan, 1950.

DAVIS, W. HERSEY. *Beginner's Grammar of the Greek New Testament.* New York: Harper and Brothers Publishers, n.d.

ELLIOTT, L.R. *Syntax in Diagram.*

GILES, P. *A Short Manual for Students of Comparative Philology.* Second Edition, Revised. London: Macmillan and Co., Ltd., 1901.

GREEN, SAMUEL G. *Handbook to the Grammar of the Greek New Testament*. Second Edition, Revised. N.p.: The Religious Tract Society, n.d.

JESPERSEN, OTTO. *The Philosophy of Grammar*. London: George Allen and Unwin, Ltd., 1951.

KITTEL, GERHARD and FRIEDRICK, GERHARD (eds.). *Theological Dictionary of the New Testament*. Trans. by GEOFFREY W. BROMILEY. Grand Rapids: Eerdmans.

KÜHNER, RAPHAEL. *Grammar of the Greek New Testament*. Trans. by B. B. Edwards and S. H. Taylor. Eighth Edition. New York: D. Appelton and Co., 1888.

MACHEN, J. GRESHAM. *New Testament Greek for Beginners*. New York: The MacMillan Company, 1960.

MOORHOUSE, A.C. *Studies in the Greek Negative*. Cardiff: University of Wales Press, 1959.

MOULE, C.F.D. *An Idiom Book of New Testament Greek*. Second Edition. Cambridge: University Press, 1963.

MOULTON, J. H. *A Grammar of New Testament Greek*. Vol. I *Prolegomena*. Third Edition. Edinburgh: T. & T. Clark, 1908.

MOULTON, J.H. and HOWARD, W. F. *A Grammar* . . . . Vol. II. *Accidence and Word-Formation*. Edinburgh: T. & T. Clark, n.d.

MOULTON, J.H. and TURNER, NIGEL. *A Grammar* . . . . Vol. III.

————. *A Grammar* . . . . Vol. IV. *Style*. Edinburgh: T. & T. Clark. 1976.

NUNN, H. P. V. *A Short Syntax of New Testament Greek*. Second Edition. Cambridge: The University Press.

ROBERTSON, A.T. *A Grammar of the Greek New Testament in the Light of Historical Research*. Fourth Edition. Nashville: Broadman Press, 1923.

ROBERTSON, A.T. and DAVIS, W. HERSEY. *A New Short*

Grammar of the Greek New Testament. Tenth Edition.
New York: Harper and Brothers Publishers, n.d.

SUMMERS, RAY. *Essentials of New Testament Greek.* Nashville:
Broadman Press, 1950.

THRALL, MARGARET E. *Greek Particles in the New Testament.*
Leiden: E. J. Birll, 1962.

THUMB, A. *Handbook of the Modern Greek Varnacular:
Grammar, Texts, Glossary.* Trans. by S. Angus. Second
Edition. Edinburgh: T. & T. Clark, 1912.

ZERWICK, MAXIMILIAN. *Biblical Greek.* Trans. by JOSEPH SMITH.
Rome: Scripta Pontificii Instituti Biblici, 1963.

Commentaries

BEARE, F. W. *The First Epistle of Peter: The Greek Text with
Introduction and Notes.* Second Edition, Revised.
Oxford: Basil Blackwell, 1961.

BIGG, C. *The Epistles of St. Peter and St. Jude* in
"International Critical Commentary." Edinburgh: T. &
T. Clark, 1901.

CRANFIELD, C. E. B. *I & II Peter and Jude: Introduction and
Commentary.* London: SCM Press, 1960.

FRAME, J. E. *A Critical and Exegetical Commentary on the
Epistles of St. Paul to the Thessalonians* in "International
Critical Commentary." Edinburgh: T. & T. Clark, 1912.

HORT, F. J. A. *The First Epistle of St. Peter: i:1-ii:17.* London:
Macmillan & Co., 1898.

KELLEY, J. N. D. *A Commentary on the Epistles of Peter and of
Jude* in "Harper's New Testament Commentaries." New
York: Harper & Row, 1969.

MILLIGAN, GEORGE. *St. Paul's Epistles to the Thessalonians:
The Greek Text with Introduction and Notes.* Reprint
Edition. Grand Rapids: Wm. B. Eerdmans, 1952.

MORRIS, L. *The Epistles of Paul to the Thessalonians: An*

Introduction and Commentary. Grand Rapids: Wm B. Eerdmans, 1957.

————. *The First and Second Epistles to the Thessalonians* in "The New International Commentary on the New Testament." Grand Rapids: Wm. B. Eerdmans, 1959.

ROBERTSON, A. T. *Word Pictures in the New Testament.* Six Volumes. Nashville: Broadman Press, 1930-33.

SELWYN, E. G. *The First Epistle of St. Peter: The Greek Text with Introduction, Notes and Essays.* London: Macmillan, 1969.